ANTI-
TERRORISM
101:

A PRIMER
FOR
PROTECTION

By L. THOME

CHAMPAIGN COUNTY LIBRARY
1060 SCIOTO STREET
URBANA, OHIO 43078
937-653-3811

Copyright © 2001 TDM Publishing

All rights reserved. No part of this book may be reproduced or transmitted in any form or by any means, electronic or mechanical, including photocopying, recording, or by any information storage and retrieval system, without permission in writing from the publisher.

Published by TDM Publishing, PO Box 1600, McKinney, TX 75070

Printed in the U.S.A.

ISBN 1-882330-67-6

CONTENTS

INTRODUCTION

Following the 1993 bombing of the World Trade Center, I contacted John Mann, the former National Director of Wackenhut Investigations, a division of Wackenhut Corporation headquartered in Florida, with the intent of possibly doing an article for a business publication for whom I had written previously.

"Is this something we can expect to happen again?", I asked. According to Mann, whose experience, among other things, involved counter terrorist operations, Americans tended to view these acts as isolated incidents. In his estimation, quite the contrary was true. "Unfortunately, terrorists are now within U.S. shores," he said. "I think, if anything, terrorist activity will probably increase rather than decrease. It's vital that we understand this and learn how to effectively deal with it."

Sadly, Mann was correct. When terrorists did rear their ugly heads again on domestic soil, it was in the most unexpected and horrifying way. Like most citizens of this country, my husband and I watched our television with feelings of great distress as scenes of the tragic events of September 11, 2001 were shown. We could, government officials later warned, expect more attacks and more casualties in America. As one broadcast journalist succinctly commented, "Our carefree days are now over."

The public was both shocked and terrified. This was not a conventional war. It was something disturbingly new to them and they expressed frustration at not knowing how to effectively deal with the possibility of nuclear, biological or chemical terrorism. What, they worried, could average citizens do to protect themselves?

In the aftermath of the attacks on America, this book then had its genesis. In its pages, you will find considerable information that will help you to help protect yourself, your family and your business in these unfortunate and uncertain times.

In addition to an overview of terrorism, you will find the following:

- Risk analysis questionnaires for both personal and business use

- Information on how to develop a security and protection plan

- Information on terrorist surveillance detection and pre-incident indicators

- Discussion of what protective mechanism the federal government has and how the various agencies work with state and local entities in the event of a terrorist incident or attack

- Discussion of Weapons of Mass Destruction (the government's definition may surprise you)

- Definitive information on how to create a Survival Kit, including a list of the specific items you will need

- Discussion of chemical and biological terrorism, with a listing of symptoms and treatment modalities

- Discussion of nuclear and radiological terrorism, including what experts believe to be the most probable methods of delivery

- Discussion of what to do in the event of a nuclear or radiological incident or attack, including possible contamination pathways, protective action measures, the most common decontamination method, and the steps you will need to take if authorities call for an evacuation. Terms you might hear if this were to happen are also offered.

- A listing of General Emergency Preparedness Guidelines, including topics such as food storage, water purification, and a myriad of other important information

While the terrorist threat is real and frightening, there are nonetheless many measures that can be taken to mitigate it. My hope is that the information and the recommendations presented in this book will provide the necessary tools to do just that.

As with the creation of any book, there are those instrumental people who need to be acknowledged. Since the inception of this one, I have had a lot of help and encouragement from my husband Daryl and from others who willingly gave of their time and suggestions. It is to them and to you, the reader, that this book is therefore dedicated.

UNDERSTANDING THE ENEMY CONFRONTING US

"So it is said: know your enemy and know yourself; in one hundred
battles you will never be in peril; if you do not know others but
know yourself, you will be imperiled in every single battle"

-Sun Tzu, 510 B.C.

With surprisingly little fanfare, Chicago's Emergency Response and Research Institute (ERRI) issued a worldwide terrorist advisory on March 5, 2001. Regarding the report, terrorist expert Clark Staten, ERRI's Executive Director and Senior Analyst, explained, "Given the current tactical circumstances in the Mid East and the ever escalating rhetoric by various militant organizations, we feel that we must urge additional caution and awareness for Americans everywhere at this time."

Two months later, during the week of May 15th, congressional hearings on domestic terrorism exposed a litany of worries, including chemical, biological, nuclear, and cyber-terrorism designed to disrupt governmental and civil operations.

The message was a chilling one: The potential for terrorist attack was unquestionably strong. Yet no one anticipated the horrifying attacks that would take place in this country only a short time later.

From a military standpoint, the terrorists attacks on America on September 11, 2001 were clearly well-planned and well-executed. But what was equally troubling is the fact that intelligence reports indicated that more were to come. As one broadcast journalist succinctly commented, "Our carefree days are over."

Americans were deeply shocked by the brutality and devastation of the attacks, their long-held sense of security forever shattered. How, they wondered, could this have possibly happened here? And who were these terrorist monsters who had so little regard for the sanctity of human life?

Interestingly enough, several months following the bombing of the World Trade Center on February 26, 1993, an article on terrorism in TIME magazine carried this warning: "There is almost sure to be a next time - and then another and another. The end of the cold war and the disintegration of Soviet-bloc governments that often abetted terrorism have not done away with the phenomenon. Quite the opposite: terrorism of new varieties seems to be on the rise around the world. As the World Trade Center plot and last week's arrests illustrate, the U.S. is not safe any longer."

In order to understand the enemy and the threat we now face, we need to better understand this new breed of terrorism. We need to understand what motivates terrorists, as well as the ways in which they typically operate.

The United States, the only real remaining superpower, has long been a primary target of international terrorism, though major attacks had formerly always taken place on foreign soil. Despite the fact that the U.S. ranks among the highest of the industrialized nations in terms of crimes and homicides and despite the fact that it has one of the highest rates of legal and illegal weapons possession by its citizens, it has

rarely seen politically motivated terrorist attacks until fairly recently.

There are a number of contributing factors, but one of the more obvious reason

is that America is such an ethnically and politically absorptive society. Much to the

dismay of our enemies and violent irridentist groups, we have continually demonstrated

unwavering political and economic stability, religious freedom, and a high degree of

social mobility. These attributes, that are wonderfully idiosyncratic to this country, have

thus established the United States as both a reason for hope and a reason for hate.

Heightened global unrest, military retaliatory actions, as well as unrelenting

political and religious extremism have exacerbated terrorism's threat. Indeed,

bombings, assassinations, hijackings, extortion attempts, kidnappings, and disruption of

governmental and business operations are terrorist activities that became increasingly

common in this generation. In 1990, for example, Business Risks International

recorded 3,969 acts of terrorism around the world, many of which were directed

at businesses or their executives. By 1992, Pinkerton Risk Assessment Services

concluded that terrorist attacks worldwide increased to a record 5,404 and that

the number of people killed rose to above 10,000 for the first time. While Pinker-

ton is perhaps more liberal than others in that it used a much broader definition of

terrorism that included violent acts committed inside a country by its own citizens,

the statistics are nonetheless compelling.

Terrorism emerged from the cradle of civilization in the Middle East and, while there have been changes in technology and geopolitical scenarios, we find that many of the basic motivational elements and tactics that existed then remain the same today.

One of the earliest recorded terrorist events took place around 6 BC. Jews had suffered for years under highly oppressive Roman rule. Realizing that the prospects for any substantive improvement were dim, a Jewish revolutionary sect known as the Zealots decided to take aggressive action. Through the use of an assassin squad called the Sicarii (named after the particular dagger they used), the group systematically eliminated high profile senators, judges, centurions and any others they deemed guilty.

Walter Laquer, in his book The Age of Terrorism, mentioned that another group, the Assassins, appeared in the eleventh century. An offshoot of the Ismailis, he said they have fascinated Western authorities for a long time due to the fact that some of the features of this movement are reminiscent of current terrorist movements. Based in Persia, the Assassins spread to Syria. Said Laquer, "Their first leader, Hassan Sibai, seems to have realized early on that his group was too small to confront the enemy in open battle but that a planned, systematic, long-term campaign of terror carried out by a small, disciplined force could be the most effective political weapon." In 1991, the Gulf War again brought this realization to Middle Eastern dissident groups.

Laquer wrote that "After World War I, it became the fashion among some governments to finance terrorist groups; thus the Italians and the Hungarians gave money to the Croats and the Macedonian IMRO (44 million lira in 1929-33). IMRO also received funds from the Bulgarians, and the Poles allegedly at one time paid the Rumanian Iron Guard, though this has not been proven. This fashion became even more popular after the Second World War, and with the rise of international and state-sponsored terrorism, the amounts changing hands amounted to many millions."

More recently, in the 1980's and 1990's, the names and activities of terrorists or terrorist groups such as Abu Nidal, Carlos, the Red Brigade, the Shining Path, the IRA, PLO, the Islamic Resistance Movement (or Hamas, as it is also called) and the HizbAllah became well known to us from newspaper headlines. In fact, Libyan strongman Moammar Gadhafi got worldwide attention when it was learned that he sent his hit squads to seven different countries to carry out 14 attacks against Libyan exiles who opposed his regime. Eleven were said to have been murdered outright.

In another instance, in 1989, German businessman Alfred Herrhausen, the highly regarded and influential head of the Deutsch Bank, was being driven home in his armored Mercedes-Benz, when terrorists struck. Herrhausen was assassinated and his driver severely injured when a bomb hidden beneath a nearby bicycle was triggered by a light beam positioned approximately 660 feet away from it. The West German terrorist group, the Red Army Faction, took credit for the carnage.

For observers of such things, the 1980's marked a change in terrorism. Although some may argue to the contrary, considerable evidence surfaced that seemed

to suggest a growing commonality among the various groups worldwide at this time.

For example, many of the violent acts of terrorism that took place previously appeared

to be carried out by a somewhat diverse group of perpetrators espousing a variety of

seemingly unrelated causes. Too, they typically showed varying degrees of ability and

sophistication in terms of how they executed their strikes.

In contrast, around the start of the 1980's, international terrorist efforts began to

exhibit considerable tactical skill and a mastery of complex and, in many cases, highly

advanced technologies. What was particularly troublesome, however, was <u>the fact</u>

<u>that increasing numbers of these groups appeared to be unusually well-coordinated</u>

<u>and extremely well funded</u>. Lastly, with the exception of some of the more parochial

or ethnically-oriented groups, the almost universal goal of these modern terrorists was

to target the "Great White Satan" of the West and its Judeo-Christian values. Israel,

Western Europe, Canada, and the United States thus became the unwilling recipients

of this violent discontent.

Yossef Bodansky, former Director of the House Republican Task Force on

Terrorism and Unconventional Warfare, brought up an interesting point in his earlier

book, <u>Target America: Terrorism in the U.S. Today.</u> "This fact must be emphatically

understood," he says, "...none of the rage of the Third World, and especially the Muslim

world, could have been transformed into the sophisticated and lethal extremist violence

12

the West is currently facing had it not been for the comprehensive support and funding

provided to international terrorism by Iran, Syria, Sudan, and a myriad of allies and

proxies. And despite the much-heralded recent changes in Eastern Europe and the

Soviet Union, the death of Khomeini and the hope for more 'moderate' successors such

as Hashemi-Rafsanjani, Assad's apparent rallying to the US-sponsored peace process,

the relative silence of Qaddafi and other seeming changes, behind the scenes these

activities have not ceased. On the contrary, as noted above, preparations are now well

underway to escalate the terrorist struggle and bring the battle to American soil."

Islamic fundamentalists, Bodansky accurately concluded, had embarked on a

holy war -or Jihad - against the West which would rapidly replace and possibly surpass

the threat formerly posed by Marxism. Further, he felt that the sponsoring states were

covertly endeavoring to solicit support from other terrorist groups internationally and

from disgruntled elements within American society by providing considerable funding for

their individual operations. Citing mounting evidence, including written material by

highly placed Islamic fundamentalists, he correctly predicted that the 1993 bombing of

the World Trade Center and subsequent activities were merely a prelude to a virulent

campaign against the West, much of which would be played in this country.

U.S. News & World Report confirmed almost as much in its September 20,1993

issue which discussed the disturbing rise of terrorism in the United States. "The

number and diversity of the radical Islamic and Palestinian organizations operating here is dizzying", it said. "The Islamic Committee for Palestine, for example, is based in Tampa, Florida . Two conferences sponsored by the organization featured representatives of the fanatic Palestinian Islamic Jihad organization among its principal speakers. The group's spiritual leader, Sheik Abd al-Aziz Odeh, addressed the gathering with Rachid al-Ghanouchi, the leader of Tunisa's outlawed al-Nahda Party, which is financed by the government of Sudan. Despite these links, spokesmen for the Islamic Committee deny any ties to the Islamic Jihad, which has claimed responsibility for terrorist attacks and kidnappings in the Middle East."

Along with Tampa, Detroit and Dearborn, Michigan were cited in the article as cities where radical fundamentalist elements had set up shop, although other sources also mentioned Los Angeles, San Francisco, and several more areas as probable cell domiciles. According to Bodansky and others, in fact, imported terrorist "dormant cells" had been firmly established and mainstreamed into the American community since at least the early to mid-1980's. They reported further that highly trained individual terrorist plants, often referred to as "submarines", had been strategically placed in government, and business and industry, not only for the purpose of information gathering, but to facilitate implementation of a strike when the time was deemed appropriate.

According to the U.S. News & World Report article cited earlier, "Israel security sources say another Palestinian arrested recently testified that he and other young

14

enthusiasts received bomb training at a secret session of a pro-Hamas conference in Kansas City, Mo. FBI officials initially discounted reports of Hamas activity. U.S. News has learned, however, that the FBI has recently intensified its investigation of pro-Hamas organizations in America."

Articles appearing in the mid-1980's in both the Washington Times and the Washington Post indicate that more than100 well-trained Shiite terrorists were already deployed within the U.S., having entered through Mexico. According to the articles, these entities were harbored primarily by students from Muslim countries, the population of which was cited at approximately 60,000 at that time. Additionally, several Iranian "students", studying in this country on scholarships from Tehran, returned to Iran on a periodic basis for further military training. After returning here, they allegedly resumed their studies and generally avoided participation in major clandestine operations. Instead, they acted as "sleeper agents" waiting for activation as needed.

It probably comes as no surprise that North Korea, as well as the former Soviet Union and other Eastern Block countries, previously provided Middle Eastern terrorists (and presumably others) with expert training in such areas as intelligence, terrorism, and subversion. To be more specific, some of the course offerings included nuclear, biological, and chemical warfare, production of incendiary devices, bridge destruction, and considerable other useful information. Zehdi Terzi, the PLO's UN representative, in an interview for a PBS documentary on terrorism in 1979, admitted, "Our boys go to the Soviet Union. They go everywhere for their training, for their education; there is no secret about that."

Between 1981 and 1985 alone, the Iranian terrorist training system is said to have turned out roughly 3,000 individuals to act as operatives. The largest of their schools during this period, the Manzarieh Park camp in Tehran, apparently included facilities for training suicide missions.

Terrorist instruction manuals have recently surfaced, among them the 11-volume "Manual of Afghan Jihad". It is interesting to note that the volumes were obtained by the Associated Press from a former Afghan fighter who reportedly got them from a Libyan fighter. He reported that the Libyan apparently had a "falling out" with his comrades and somehow managed to steal the volumes from the headquarters of Osama bin Laden's organization in Kandahar.

Ranging in length from 250 to 500 pages, the volumes provide explicit information on such topics as explosives handling and manufacturing, how to drive a tank, and how to deal with everything from electric shocks to brain hemorrhages and typhoid.

In discussing security and intelligence, the authors said, "In preparedness for war, security and intelligence gathering of the enemy's power and strategy have been emphasized in accordance to the instructions of the Quran."

The chapter on "basic sabotage and destruction", provides the "holy warriors" with a variety of options such as "poison-making, poisonous gases, and poisonous drugs." They even instruct that a particular odorless gas will, in fact, kill a person in 30 seconds.

Most interesting perhaps, in light of the methods used by the airline highjackers during the September 11, 2001 attacks, is the volume on hand-to-hand combat, which includes a chapter on "how to threaten with a knife, piercing with a knife."

Another instruction manual, written for Muslim operatives and not among those in the 11-volume set, was discovered in 2000 during an investigation being conducted into the activities of bin Laden at that time.

Bloodshed and violence are not the only things in the terrorist repertoire, however. For instance in the 1970's, the PLO's Yasir Arafat and his lieutenants, in order to feed his secret discretionary fund, operated a multinational crime syndicate which utilized such tactics as extortion, bribery, narcotics trafficking, and murder. Inside the PLO, by Neil C. Livingstone and David Halevy, reported that "At least four European airlines reportedly took advantage of the PLO's 'flight insurance' program. Most, it is presumed, decided that it was cheaper to pay protection money than to install comprehensive security measures. Lufthansa joined the 'program' after one of its planes had been hijacked by the PFLP to Aden in February 1972. After paying the PFLP five million dollars for the release of the plane and passengers, Lufhansa annually shelled out five to ten million to elements within the PLO for immunity from further attacks. The money went into the Chairman's Secret Fund and was divided up among the number of Palestinian terrorist groups, including the PFLP. This system remained in place until a Lufthansa jetliner was seized by terrorists in 1977 and ultimately diverted to Mogadishu, Somalia, where it was later stormed by West German GSG-9 commandos. Lufthansa subsequently declined to pay further 'protection' money to the PLO."

In the 1990's Syrian-inspired counterfeiting efforts to flood the U.S. and global market with high quality, but decidedly fake $100 bills demonstrated the incredible skill with which current terrorist groups now operate. The bills were so well-rendered, even Treasury Department experts had trouble recognizing them. The objectives appear to have been the destabilization of the U.S. economy and also to help fund terrorists with their continual purchases of high tech weaponry. But consider another scenario brought up in a Department of Defense anti-terrorist handbook: "Use of sophisticated computer viruses introduced into computer-controlled systems for banking, information, communications, life support and manufacturing could result in massive disruptions of highly organized technological societies." The consequences here, of course, are significant at best.

According to Bodansky, the Iranian-Syrian long-term strategy of which he became aware involved a three-phase strategy based on a gradual escalation of terrorist strikes that would put to test the extent and effectiveness of the reaction of American law enforcement authorities. As he explained, "The three phases of the Iranian-Syrian long-term terrorist strategy were as follows:

1. Use of local expendable assets to carry out operations while creating problems for the local security forces;

2. Quality attacks by operative already on site, living off of and gaining operational support from the locally based dormant networks; an

3. Spectacular strikes, including suicide strikes, by specially placed expert terrorists in order to demonstrate the global reach of the Iran-led Muslim Bloc and to avenge the Muslim world."

Further, Bodansky, says, a separate terrorist system was supposed to be introduced with each phase in order to complicate the ability of law enforcement agencies to identify a pattern. Add to that Moammar Qaddif's disturbing statement made in 1984 that "We must force America to fight on 100 fronts all over the earth, in Lebanon, in Chad, in Sudan, in El Salvador, in Africa" and the scope and seriousness of the new breed of terrorism became startlingly evident.

During the 1980's a new face entered the terrorism realm. In 1979 the Soviet invasion of Afghanistan prompted Osama bin Laden to leave his home in Saudi Arabia to join the Afghan resistance (Mujahedeen). In 1988, bin Laden, who by this time had emerged as a leader in the resistance movement, had already established the now well-known al Qaeda organization, the intent of which was to funnel support and financial assistance to the Afghan resistance. Mort Rosenblum, in September 23, 2001 Associated Press report, explained that "During the 1980's, the United States supported several ragtag rebel groups eager to fight the Soviet Union in Afghanistan. Americans provided funds and arms, including Stringer surface-to-air missiles." While bin Laden denies receiving any CIA funds directly, it is a well-established fact that he did indeed receive American logistical and political support.

After the withdrawal of Soviet troops from Afghanistan, bin Laden returned to Saudi Arabia a folk hero. Yet it was only a short time later before he was forced to flee his home and return to Afghanistan as a result of his strong opposition to the Saudi alliance with the United States during the Gulf War. He was further enraged that American troops had set foot in what were considered Islamic Holy sites.

By now, the shape and scope of the still active al Qaeda had significantly changed, its hatred of the West intensified. Through its leader bin Laden, al Qaeda appealed to other terrorist organizations to cooperate in the fight against its common enemy, the United States. Then, in 1998, he issued a declaration or fatwah with the World Muslim Front" stating that it was a Muslim's duty to kill Americans, including civilians, anywhere in the world. In addition to al Qaeda, members of this front reportedly included the Egyptian Jihad, the Pakistani Society of Ulemas, the Ansar Movement, the Bangladesh Jihad and the Islamic Army for The Liberation of Holy Sites.

New recruits were drafted from a variety of sources, including religious schools. The reward for joining the jihad, bin Laden said, was an honored place in paradise, in accordance with the Quran that states, "a martyr's privileges are guaranteed by Allah".

A September 23, 2001 article by Washington Post writer Michael Dobbs reported, "In the 10 years before his emergence Sept. 11 as the prime suspect in the deadliest terrorist attack in history, the 44-year old bin Laden has described his goals, grievances and tactics in great detail in a series of statements and interviews. Taken together, these statements provide insights into an ideology that seems abhorrent and even crazy to the vast majority of Americans but has been crafted carefully to appeal to the disgruntled and dispossessed of the Islamic world."

The article's sidebar reported that "Today, some Muslims say they are again under Western siege. The global economy driven by the West has created new desires and new pressures. Liberal ideas associated with the West are spread through television, movies and popular music - an emphasis on individual choice that weakens male authority, the mixing of men and women at school and at work, frank discussion of sex."

The sidebar also stated that "The overriding concern, however, is the conflict that has been fought since the creation in 1948 of Israel as a haven for persecuted Jews on their biblical land. Israel statehood made hundred of thousands of Palestinians, most of them Muslim, homeless."

Regardless of the brand of terrorism involved, there are certain common denominators that exist regarding the terrorist mentality. For one thing, terrorists seem universally not to regard themselves as aggressors, but rather as saviors for an oppressed people. Also, a strong sense of victimization is usually present and with it a very narrow or parochial definition of what constitutes justice or vindication. It's fair to say, too, that those who have grown up in an environment of continual conflict, such as that experienced in the Middle East for example, tend to consider violence as a justifiable means of expression. It's important to remember, too, that in many Third-World countries taking up arms is considered a rite of passage into manhood. Further, in many of these same countries, there is a strong history of tribal blood feuds involving hostage taking, hostage trading, assassination, and other forms of revenge that have frequently continued for centuries, with little indication of cessation. Examples of this may be found both in the Middle East and in some of the Eastern bloc countries. There is often a generational legacy of violence, then, with which we must contend.

Of course there are other distinctions, but experts point out that in the case of Muslim fundamentalists, there are a combination of factors at play: political, religious, and fanatical. For this group, there is no separation of church and state. Further, it's important to keep in mind that these individuals hold a significantly different view of life and afterlife than those of us in the West. As we have learned, a sincere belief predominates among the Muslim devout that self-sacrifice in the name of Allah of the jihad will guarantee passage into heaven or paradise.

It's important to understand that Muslim (or Islamic) fundamentalists are not representative of all Muslims and are certainly not representative of all Middle Easterners. Nonetheless, the combination of religious and political fervor exhibited by the Muslim fundamentalists does seem to result in the breeding of highly dedicated terrorists who are both murderous and suicidal.

Michael Papa, the former director of the United States Navy mine action program in Afghanistan, and one of the last American citizens to have spent any significant time in that county, reported in a September 30, 2001 email to former fellow United States Military Academy graduates that the mine action program is "the most respected relief effort in the country and because of this I had the opportunity to travel extensively, without too much interference restriction.'

Papa reported that the people of Afghanistan are not our enemy. He said, rather, that "... our enemy is a group of non-Afghans, often referred to as 'Arabs' and a fanatical group of religious leaders and their military cohort, the Taliban. The non-Afghan contingent came from all over the Islam world to fight in the war again the Russians. Many came using a covert network created with assistance by our own government. OBL (as Osama bin Laden was referred to by us in the country at the time) restored this network to bring in more fighters, this time to support the Taliban in their civil war against the former Mujehdeen. Over time this military support along with financial support has allowed OBL and his 'Arabs' to co-op significant government activities and leaders. OBL is the "inspector general" of Taliban armed forces, his body guards protect senior Taliban leaders and he has built a system of deep bunkers for the Taliban which were designed to withstand cruise missile strikes (uhm where did he learn to do that?) His forces basically rule the southern city of Kandahar."

Shortly after the 1993 World Trade Center bombing, Libyan strongman Moammar Gadhafi, in an interview in the Washington Times, made this thought-provoking statement: "Acts of terrorism in America are the answer and they will be more and more violent and spectacular for television purposes around the world."

Unfortunately, Americans have often had the tendency to assume that the values they hold are universal values held by all human kind. History has repeatedly shown us that this is not the case. The concepts we have of democracy, of freedom in its many forms, of human rights, of brotherhood, and of gender equality are not necessarily embraced by other cultures. This has become increasingly evident over the past few years. The question now, of course, is where and when will terrorists strike next?

The answer to this can be found by looking more closely at how terrorists think and how they have operated in the recent past. Writing in October 2001 for the Center for Defense Information, Senior Analyst Nicolas Berry noted that terrorists seek to weaken their enemy by relying on the use and threat of violence. He pointed out that, while their targets are the political authority, "Civilians are easier to attack and often produce dramatic consequences."

Berry explained further that, by their attacks, terrorists seek to prove that the political authority cannot protect its own population, cannot protect society's institutions, cannot protect society's infrastructure, and, among other things, cannot maintain normal, peaceful conditions in society. He believes that they seek to produce these effects by attacking such targets as important government and civilian buildings and monuments, key factories and businesses including banks, transportation and communication networks, and utilities.

Berry mentioned that in selecting their targets, terrorists concern themselves with the element of surprise in the attack, which they hope will cause panic and paralysis in the citizenry, the drama of the attack, which they hope will cause awe and fixation, the availability of media to publicize the attacks and other factors.

In addressing the nation following the September 11, 2001 attacks, President George Bush emphasized that we face a new kind of war, one which may take years to fight. "Make no mistake," he said, " the United States will hunt down and punish those responsible for these cowardly acts." He stated further that the United States would make no distinction between those who committed the crime and those who harbor them."

While endorsing steps being taken by the Bush administration to protect our borders and to engage this unseen enemy in a new kind of war, privately many

Americans worry about how they can protect themselves, their families, and their

businesses. Secretary of Defense Donald Rumsfield warned that American must

expect retaliation as the war on terrorism steps up. Yet how do we as private citizens

protect ourselves from this unseen threat?

UNDERSTANDING THE TERRORIST THREAT AND THE RISKS WE FACE

*"Blandishments will not fascinate us nor will threats
of a 'halter' intimidate. For under God, we are determined
that wheresoever, whensoever, or howsoever we shall
be called upon to make our exit, we will die free men"*

- Observations from the Boston Port Bill (1774)

For most of us, the term "terrorism" previously evoked mental images of shadowy figures stealthily at work on nefarious deeds. In many cases, these images were generated as a result of watching television coverage of world news events like the 1988 bombing of Pan Am flight 103 or from reading engaging, suspense-filled books of fiction like The Fifth Horseman by Larry Collins and Dominique LaPierre. In either case, while we may since have developed a much more accurate and personal understanding of terrorism, the realization that terrorists may have been living next door or frequenting the same stores and restaurants probably never entered our consciousness. Indeed, the startling realization that terrorists were no longer "out there" but among us has given us all pause for thought.

In the highly intriguing document, Revolutionary Catechism, written in the 19th century by Russian nihilists Mikhail Bakunin and Serge Nechaev, the authors made this interesting, though disturbing, point: "The revolutionary knows that in the very depths of his being he has broken all ties with society, both in word and in deed. He breaks all ties with the civilized world, its laws, its customs, its morality, all those conventions generally accepted by the world. He is their implacable enemy, and if he has intercourse with the world, it is only for the purpose of destroying it."

As a direct result of the noticeable increase in terrorism in the 1980's and 1990's, including the World Trade Center bombing in 1993, the Presidential Directive (PDD) - 39, "U.S. Policy on Counterterrorism" was issued. This policy, signed by President Clinton on June 21, 1995, established that acts of terrorism would be considered both a threat to national security and a criminal act, and that all such acts against our country or its citizens would merit a vigorous response.

Four basic concepts were set forth in PDD-39:

- Reduce U.S. vulnerability to terrorist attacks

- Deter terrorist attacks before they occur

- Respond vigorously to terrorist attacks that may take place

- Develop effective capabilities to address the threat of weapons of mass destruction (WMD)

PDD-39 delineates the goals and responsibilities of the many agencies involved in this counter-terrorism effort, with the Federal Bureau of Investigation (FBI) being the Lead Federal Agency for all domestic terrorist events.

The "Defense Against Weapons of Mass Destruction Act of 1996", also referred to as the Nunn-Lugar-Domenici Act, augmented PDD-39 by working to improve our ability to respond to the threats of nuclear, radiological, chemical, or biological incidents.

As the shock and horror from the catastrophic terrorist attacks on the World Trade Center and Pentagon gave way to the grim reality that more attacks could be expected, government agencies scrambled to respond. New and greater concerns emerged over the vulnerability of America's infrastructure, its transportation and communication networks, as well as its utilities, and manufacturing plants. In addition, all high profile businesses, perhaps especially the multinationals having headquarters in the United States, were thought to be conceivable targets.

Anthony H. Cordesman, Burke Chair Holder, Center for Strategic and International Studies, testifying before the Senate Judiciary Subcommittee on Technology, Terrorism, and Government Information, stated on March 27, 2001 that "We need to conduct and systematically update our analysis of the vulnerability of our critical infrastructure, including financial systems, information systems, communication systems, utilities, and transportation nets and make sure our intelligence can focus on potential threats."

According to Cordesman, too, "Advances in biotechnology, food processing equipment, pharmaceuticals, and other dual-use facilities and technologies are also proliferating at a civil level and becoming steadily more available to governments, extremist movements, and individuals. These problems are compounded by the rapid spread of expertise and equipment for genetic engineering. The end result is that the technology of attacks on humans, livestock, and crops is becoming more available, and in forms which not only can be extremely lethal and/or costly, but difficult to attribute to a given attacker."

More recently, concern has mounted over the fact that the nation's immigration tracking system is desperately in need of restructuring. "Our nation is best characterized as a sieve," said Dianne Feinstein, D-California and an immigration subcommittee member. "Clearly people are exploring the penetration points of our system to put themselves in close touch with either substances or instruments of mass destruction in the United States."

As was pointed out in Chapter One, both the Washington Times and the Washington Post reported as early as the mid-1980's, that foreign students from Muslim countries have been harboring terrorists, many of whom entered through Mexico. Yet the Immigration and Naturalization Service (INS) reportedly is unable to track more than half a million of these foreign students.

A disturbing October 7, 2001 Washington Post article by Steve Fainaru and Gilbert M. Gaul, stated that "The concerns peaked in 1993 with the revelations that the terrorist who drove an explosive-filled truck under the World Trade Center arrived on a visa to study engineering at Wichita State University.'

"In 1995," they continue, "an INS task force concluded that the agency 'has no system in place to monitor or audit schools' and did not know when foreign students depart, drop out, transfer, interrupt their education, violate statues or otherwise violate the law."

According to the article, "By 1996, Congress ordered the INS to update computerized tracking of foreign students. After the agency launched a 21-school experiment, colleges protested that student tracking would stigmatize foreigners and impose a burdensome $95 fee."

Keep in mind that before his arrival in this country, the Egyptian-born Mohammed Atta, one of the hijackers suspected to have been responsible for the 2001 attacks, previously lived in Hamburg, Germany where he was believed to have been a part of a "student" cell. Although Atta arrived in this country on a tourist visa and would therefore not have been officially listed as a student, he was of course among one of the large number of pilot trainees we know to exist. So certainly student tracking is not the only challenge to the INS. Still, the knowledge that Osama bin Laden's younger brother had been a student at Harvard University aroused attention, despite whether he actually participated in any terrorist activity or not.

Gaps appear to exist not only in INS dealings, but also with respect to criminal statutes and certain aspects of law enforcement. The issue, of course, is how to combat the threat of further domestic terrorism without significantly altering the civil liberties and freedoms Americans have so long enjoyed. Wiretap laws to accommodate recent technological advances such as the internet and email, pagers, and cell phones are under review. In the meantime, surveillance and other investigative methods being used under current law to counter terrorism mean that FBI and police officials must continue to walk a fine line in order to protect this nation's assets and population. It is vital, therefore, that citizens educate themselves as to the issues. It is also vital that they understand the role they must play both in national and personal security.

An October 6, 2001 Washington Post article by Susan Schmidt and Bob Woodward stated that, based on what officials described as "credible" information, U.S. intelligence officials, in a report to Congress, indicated that there was a high probability that terrorists associated with bin Laden would try to launch another major attack on the U.S. either here or abroad. The concern, based on intelligence gathered from England, Germany, Afghanistan, and Pakistan indicated that Egyptian, Somalian and Pakistani elements of bin Laden's organization were involved.

Confirming Nicholas Berry's conclusions, cited earlier, Schmidt and Woodward reported, "Government officials are fearful of attacks at any of hundreds or thousands of locations, including symbols of American power and culture, such as government buildings in Washington and centers of entertainment. They are concerned about truck bomb and car bomb explosions that could be detonated near natural gas lines, power plants and other sites that one source described as 'exposed infrastructure."

In examining the threats before us, we must, of course look at chemical, biological, and nuclear warfare. Of the three, chemical warfare may be one of the easiest in terms of being "user friendly". Fertilizer, pesticide, and seeding operations tend to be a more accessible route to obtain plant and animal toxins, and, of course, agriculture makes a very large and very good target. Nerve agents, which are lethal, blister agents, which are generally non-lethal, but very nasty, blood agents which interfere with the oxygen transfer in the bloodstream and are therefore lethal, and choking agents, which are also quite lethal, are among the arsenal that current terrorists have available.

Then there are also the chemicals such as magnesium, aluminum, phosphorous, gasoline, and petroleum distillates that can, depending on what other ingredients are combined with them, be extremely deadly. Others exist as well and, in some cases, the availability of "recipes" can be easily found on the internet. America saw an example of chemical terrorism in the senseless and tragic 1995 bombing of the Oklahoma City Federal building.

Chemical terrorism, while frightening, has some notable drawbacks in terms of delivery. It also tends to be more limited in the level of devastation it can cause. Due to the geographical enormity of the United States, to wreak the type of spectacular event Gadhafi described, chemical terrorism probably wouldn't be the first choice.

Bio-terrorism is another threat with which this country is having to deal. Like chemical warfare, biological warfare or terrorism can be expressed in a number of very unpleasant forms. These are categorized as Category A, B, and C agents, with A being

being the most dangerous.

Category A:

Bacillus anthracis (Anthrax)

Clostridium botulinum (Botulism)

Hemorrhagic fever viruses (Venezuelan Equine Encephalitis, Ebola,

Marburg, Lassa Fever)

Yersinia pestis (Plague)

Francisella tularensis (Tulemia or "rabbit fever")

Category B:

Coxiella burnetti (Q Fever)

Brucella species (Brucellosis)

Birjolderia mallei (Glanders)

Ricin toxin or Ricius communis (from Caster Bean)

Clostridium perfringens

Staphylococcal enterotoxin B

Category C:

Nipah virus

Hantaviruses

Tickborne encephalitis viruses

Yellow fever

Multi-drug resistant tuberculosis

Biological agents take the form of pathogens and toxins. Pathogens are infectious microorganisms that can cause diseases in humans, animals, and also plants. Anthrax and smallpox are an example of a pathogen. Toxins, on the other hand, are poisons which are produced by living organisms.

Biological weapons are relatively inexpensive and are fairly easy to produce or obtain. With little training or equipment, in fact, small amounts of a culture or agent could be reproduced to develop significantly larger quantities. Additionally, there are a variety of ways biological agents can be disseminated. Also, and this is an important consideration, the varying incubation periods involved, which can be from several hours to weeks, make recognition of such an attack more difficult than a chemical attack.

Biological agents would typically be disseminated in either liquid or aerosol form, although powder forms could also be used. These could be disseminated using crop dusters or other types of aircraft or, in the case of an aerosol, hidden in a briefcase or other method of disguise for use in a train station, bus station, airport or shopping mall. The problem here is that many biological agents are difficult to maintain or keep alive, bacteria like anthrax being a notable exception. Bacteria is more resistant than viruses to cold, heat, drying, chemicals, and even radiation.

Anthrax is a type of bacteria that attacks the skin, lungs, and gastrointestinal

35

tract. It occurs naturally in hoofed animals such as cattle and sheep and can be introduced into the body through cuts or abrasions. The incubation period is one to seven days and early symptoms include itching or the appearance of lesions on the skin, chills, fever, nausea and the swelling of lymph nodes. Respiratory symptoms also occur. Although it usually responds to treatment with antibiotics, if left untreated, death will follow in 24-48 hours.

Plague is another worrisome bacteria, which is normally transmitted to humans from infected rats through fleabites. There are three types of plague: bubonic, septicemic, or pneumatic. The pneumatic variety can be transmitted more covertly through the use of an aerosol spray which is inhaled into the respiratory tract.

Bubonic plague is transmitted through rats and fleas. After entering the body, the bacilli rapidly spread through the lymphatic system causing enlarged lymph nodes or buboes in the groin area. It could, however, invade the bloodstream instead, causing septicemic plague. The lungs, spleen, spinal cord and brain could also be affected. The incubation period is two to six days for bubonic plague. Fortunately, it is not directly communicable to other humans.

Pneumonic plague also spreads rapidly, after an incubation period of two to three days. Early symptoms include high fever, chills, headache, spitting up blood, and shortness of breath. Treatment with antibiotics is generally successful; however if left untreated, the disease has a mortality rate of 90 to 100%.

During World War II, the Japanese reproduced fleas in large numbers, infected them with Yersinia pestis, the bacillus responsible for bubonic plague, and then released them into several Chinese cities. Small epidemics then ensued.

What is particularly frightening is the fact that during the Cold War, the Soviet Union created a "super plague" agent which is extremely contagious and has a mortality rate of 100%.

Francisella tularensis, or tularemia (at one time called "rabbit fever") can be found in infected sheep, beaver, meadow voles, wild rabbits and squirrels. But blood sucking insects and ticks can also serve as transmitters. Illness from tularemia has an incubation period of three to six days and produces symptoms of sudden on-set fever, chills, headache, generalized muscle infection and painful joints. Additionally, an ulcer forms at the site of the bite. Typhoid is the most deadly form of tularema.

E-coli is another bacterium considered to be a possible terrorist weapon. It causes acute bloody diarrhea and abdominal cramps. There is little or no fever. Kidney problems, seizure, high blood pressure and/or blindness may result. It's typically transmitted through contaminated ground beef or unprocessed milk, although in recent years it's presence has been detected in strawberries and other food sources.

With respect to viruses, **smallpox** is among those thought to be included in the bio-terrorist arsenal. It is caused by a parasitic virus and is classified as a "crowd disease" because it only spreads between humans and survives in large, densely

37

populated areas. It is typically spread through droplets released into the air through sneezing, but it can also be spread through physical contact. Symptoms are similar to those of flu and include fever, headache and body pain. However, after two weeks, a rash will develop, with red spots appearing on the face, hands, and feet. These eventually spread to the entire body and the spots grow to pus filled lesions similar to blisters. Victims often develop pneumonia and blindness as a result of scarring of the cornea. Vaccination is, of course, available.

Marburg and **Ebola** viruses, both of which produce severe hemorrhagic fevers have recently made headlines in this country as a result of the high mortality rates that were seen in Zaire and Sudan. Though generally spread through contact with blood and other body fluids, it can also be dispersed by terrorists through aerosol use.

The incubation period for these viruses is four to sixteen days. Initial symptoms include nausea, loss of appetite and muscle aches, followed by vomiting, sore throat and abdominal pain, and diarrhea. Chest pain may also be present. Victims may become apathetic, dehydrated, and also disoriented. Most victims will develop very severe hemorrhagic problems within five to seven days, with bleeding coming from multiple sites within the lungs and gingiva, as well as the gastrointestinal tract.

Currently there is not vaccine or treatment available for these viruses. What is particularly disturbing is the fact that Soviet bioscientists have succeeded in creating a new form of a gene-mutated virus called the "**Chimera virus**", which is a combination of the Marburg and Ebola viruses and is extremely contagious. It may be spread through aerosol methods.

Toxins are non-living and poisonous substances that are produced through the metabolic activities of plants, animals, and microorganisms. Once they enter the body, symptoms appear rapidly. For example, the venom of a snake is such a toxin. Although they are not contagious, they can nonetheless be lethal or, at the very least, highly incapacitating. There are two categories of toxins: **neuro-toxins** that attack the nervous system, and **cytotoxins** that are slower acting, but present with symptoms such as vomiting, diarrhea, rashes, blisters, bleeding and general tissue deterioration.

Unfortunately, micro-encapsulation technology has made it possible to protect otherwise unstable toxins while being dispersed.

Although there are certainly others, **staphylococcus enterotoxin B** (SEB) is also worth mentioning as a possible terrorist weapon. It is produced by a bacterium and results in what we know to be food poisoning. Moreover, it is easily produced and can contaminate food and water sources. Inhalation of this agent can cause severe complications. Initial effect occur anywhere from 30 minutes to seven hours after ingestion. Symptoms include increased salivation, severe nausea, vomiting, abdominal pain, watery diarrhea, fever, lowered blood pressure and dizziness.   Although recovery generally occurs within 24 to 35 hours, death can occur due to extreme dehydration. Unfortunately SEB cannot be destroyed through normal boiling procedures, so the contamination of water supplies or food sources makes it a concern.

A week before the September 11, 2001 attacks, bio-terrorism expert Donald Henderson of Johns Hopkins University in Baltimore, Maryland, explained to the Senate Foreign Relations Committee that a payload of approximately 200 pounds of anthrax released upwind of a large American city could conceivably cause the deaths of between 130,000 and 3 million people.

"The degree of carnage is in the same range as that forecast for a hydrogen bomb. Although there is a legitimate concern as well about the possible use of chemical weapons, they are far less effective pound for pound and extremely difficult to deploy over large areas. Ten grams of anthrax can produce as many casualties as a ton of a chemical nerve agent."

Anthrax can be produced in either powder or liquid form and could be dropped from crop dusters or other small aircraft; however, some experts feel that it is very unlikely the release could effectively reach its target due to altitude, wind conditions, and various environmental factors. This is fortunate because Tommy Thompson, Secretary of the Health and Human Services Department has indicated previously that there currently are only enough doses on hand to treat 2 million Americans and there are only 15.4 million doses of smallpox vaccine.

State and local organizations have been routinely participating in preparedness exercises designed to address chemical and biological threats. Most, but certainly not all, are cognizant of the severity of the security problems that exist and they are working to effectively handle them. Yet if we look at what terrorists ultimately hope to accomplish in terms of demoralizing this nation, another avenue exits which could ultimately wreak more havoc.

Possibly a more likely scenario would be the detonation of a small, but strategic high altitude nuclear device detonated over the United States to cause widespread damage to computer chips and electronic equipment. Electromagnetic pulse, or EMP, results when tens of thousands of volts of energy are generated from a nuclear detonation. The resulting damage to electrical circuits and to domestic electronic systems could be significant. Equally disturbing is the fact that national utilities such as power and water systems are vulnerable to EMP.

In October 1999, Lowell Wood, a physicist from Lawrence Livermore National Laboratory in California, told a House Armed Services subcommittee "Special purpose nuclear warheads on a kiloton scale, can have much more EMP effect that ordinary nuclear warheads on the megaton scale. Warheads of less that 10-kiloton yields can put out very large EMP signals."

Elaborating further, Wood said "There is reason to believe that the semiconductor-based portions of our communication system, which is to say essentially all of it, would be extremely vulnerable."

Wood explained to the subcommittee that military systems and civilian passenger aircraft would be at risk. "It is probably clear that if this attack occurred at night that most of the planes, most of the civilian airliners in the air, would be lost for obvious reasons."

John Richard Thackrah, in his book, Encyclopedia Of Terrorism And Political Violence, made this point: "The rapid growth of the civilian nuclear industry, increasing traffic in plutonium-enriched uranium and radioactive waste material, the spread of nuclear technology both in the United States and other Western nations, have all increased the opportunities for terrorists to engage in some type of nuclear action."

Thackrah states further "The possibilities for action by nuclear terrorists encompass the creation of potentially alarming hoaxes, acts of low-level symbolic sabotage aimed at causing widespread casualties and damage, thefts of nuclear material or weapons, armed attacks on nuclear weapons storage sites, the dispersal of radioactive contaminants, the manufacture of home-made nuclear weapons and the detonation or threatened detonation of such devices."

The threat and danger of a nuclear attack is very real . It is well-known that in 1992 bin Laden 's Germany-based organization was thwarted in their attempt to buy highly enriched uranium, which is necessary in the creation of a nuclear device. While additional attempts have been made, it is not known conclusively whether he was ever successful. However, an October 2, 2001 report in The National Enquirer stated that former Russian security chief Alexander Lebed reported that 43 nuclear "suitcase bombs" developed for the KGB in the 1970's seem to have disappeared from their storage location.

As Thackrah, cited earlier, pointed out, "The primary attraction for terrorists in 'going nuclear' is not necessarily the fact that nuclear weapons would enable terrorists to cause mass casualties, but rather the fact that almost any terrorist action associated with the words 'atomic' or 'nuclear' automatically generates fear in the mind of the public. Terror is violence for effect and is theatre; nuclear power, whether in the form of peaceful energy or weapons, is the most potent and to may people the most sinister force known to mankind."

More than 172 attempts to smuggle radiological materials out of the former Soviet Union have been made since 1992. In many cases, these materials may still be found in unsecured facilities. In 1993, in fact, a man, appearing to be of Arab descent, bought half a kilogram of Uranium-238. In 1995, the theft of two hundred and fifty kilograms of a substance containing commercial grade uranium from a refining plan in Udmutria was reported. Moreover, in May 2000, six containers of radioactive Cesium-137 were stolen from a refinery in Volograd. On the black market, the demand for Cesium-137 is large, as it is used by terrorists in making "dirty bombs".

To address the threat of a nuclear attack or incident, the federal government has several emergency response groups that should be mentioned. The Radiological Assistance Program (RAP) assists state and local authorities in dealing with accidents

43

or incidents involving radioactive materials. The Accident Response Group (ARG) is available to respond to an accident or incident involving a U.S. nuclear weapon. The Joint Technical Operations Team (JTOT) is a Department of Energy nuclear response team that supports the Defense Department's Explosive Ordinance Disposal teams in dealing with terrorist nuclear devices. Also of interest is the Nuclear Emergency Search Team (NEST), a sort of nuclear SWAT team. The group was formed in 1975 after an extortionist threatened to blow up the city of Boston using a nuclear device.

On September 30, 2001, Secretary of Defense Donald Rumsfield warned Americans that the threat of a terrorist-inspired chemical, biological, and nuclear attack on this country is very real. That is particularly the case since the October 7, 2001 retaliatory strikes against bin Laden and his supporters in Afghanistan.

By the very nature of terrorism, it is difficult to predict what form any new attacks might take. A small nuclear device could be detonated at high altitude and create the EMP problems discussed earlier, or one could be detonated from a freighter in a crowded West Coast harbor. There could also be multiple small strikes - bridges, manufacturing plants, entertainment centers and other sites - designed to demoralize a highly mobile society.

New York Times journalist, Maureen Dowd, in a recent tongue-in-cheek column titled "Self-Absorbed Boomers Stock Up on Gas Masks", sadly trivialized the threat that citizens of this country face. 'After all these finicky years of fighting everyday germs and inevitable mortality with fancy products, Americans are now confronted with the specter

of terrorists in crop dusters and hazardous-waste trucks spreading really terrifying,

deadly toxins like plague, smallpox, blister gents, nerve gas and botulism," she said.

"Women I know in New York and Washington debate whether to order Israeli vs.

Marine Corps gas masks, and half-hour lightweight gas masks vs. $400 eight-hour gas

masks, baby gas masks and pet gas masks, with the same meticulous attention they

gave to ordering no-foam-no-fat-no whip lattes in more innocent days. They share

information on which pharmacies still have Cipro, Sitheromax and Doxycycline, all

antibiotics that can be used for anthrax, the way they once traded tips on designer shoe

bargains. They talk more now about real botulism than its trendy cosmetic derrived

botox."

Other reporters and columnists speculate on whether materialistic Americans

have the courage, strength, and resolve to weather the challenge America is now

facing, citing the fact that radical Muslims and other terrorists groups have the kind of

commitment that transcends corporeal fear. The fact is, we probably have no choice.

On October 7, 2001, America went on nationwide alert amid fears of another

domestic terrorist attack as the United States began military action against primary

targets in Afghanistan. In addressing the nation and the world, President Bush made it

very clear that the attacks were aimed at Osama bin Laden, his supporters and the

radical Islamic Taliban. Senator Richard Shelby of Alabama, the senior Republican member of the Intelligence Committee said "I don't know when or where or how, but you can just about believe that there are going to be more attacks. To lull the American people to sleep...would be a terrible thing to do."

On the date of the American response, a video tape released by an independent television network in Qatar and translated by Reuters News Service provided the following vitriolic address by bin Laden. It is worth including here in its entirety because it is indicative of the commitment of our terrorist enemy and the challenge we face:

"Here is America struck by God Almighty in one of its vital organs, so that its greatest buildings are destroyed. Grace and gratitude to God. America has been filled with horror from north to south and east to west, and thanks be to God that what America is tasting now is only a copy of what we have tasted.'

"Our Islamic nation has been tasting the same for more than 80 years, of humiliation and disgrace, its sons killed and their blood spilled, its sanctities desecrated.'

"God has blessed a group of vanguard Muslims, the forefront of Islam, to destroy America. May God bless them and allot them a supreme place in heaven, for He is the only one capable and entitled to do so. When those have stood in defense of their weak children, their brothers and sisters in Palestine and other Muslim nations, the whole world went into an uproar, the infidels followed by the hypocrites.'

"A million innocent children are dying at this time as we speak, killed in Iraq without any guilt. We hear no denunciation, we hear no edict from hereditary rulers.

In these days, Israeli tanks rampage across Palestine, in Ramalah, Rafah and Beit Jala

and many other parts of the land of Islam, and we do not hear anyone raising his voice

or reacting. But when the sword fell upon America after 80 years, hypocrisy raised its

head up high bemoaning those killers who toyed with the blood, honor, and sanctities of

Muslims.'

"The least that can be said about those hypocrites is that they are aspostates

who followed the wrong path. They backed the butcher against the victim, the

oppressor against the innocent child. I seek refuge in God against them and ask Him to

let us see them in what they deserve.'

"I say that the matter is very clear. Every Muslim after this event (should fight for

their religion), after the senior officials in the United States of America, starting with the

head of international infidels. Bush and his staff who went on a display of vanity with

their men and horses, those who turned even the countries that believe in Islam against

us - the group that resorted to God, the Almighty, the group that refuses to be subdued

in its religion.

"They have been telling the world falsehoods that they are fighting terrorism. In

a nation at the far end of the world, Japan, hundreds of thousands, young and old, were

killed and (they say) this is not a world crime. To them it is not a clear issue. A million

children (were killed) in Iraq, to them this is not a clear issue.'

"But when a few more than ten were killed in Nairobi and Dar es Salaam, Afghanistan and Iraq were bombed and hypocrisy stood behind the head of international infidels, the modern world's symbol of paganism, America, and its allies.'

"I tell them that these events have divided the world into two camps, the camp of the faithful and the camp of infidels. May God shield us and you from them.'

"Every Muslim must rise to defend his religion. The wind of faith is blowing and the wind of change is blowing to remove evil from the Peninsula of Mohammad, peace be upon him.'

"As to America, I say to it and its people a few words: I swear to God that America will not live in peace before peace reigns in Palestine, and before all the army of infidels depart the land of Mohammad, peace be upon him.'

"God is the Greatest and glory be to Islam."

Although bin Laden's rhetoric here shows some departures from his previous diatribes, particularly with respect to the Palestinian situation, the rage is clearly evident.

Interestingly, the well-known orientalist and linguist Sir Richard Burton, writing in the 1800's, commented that he always found that Arabs were very honorable. Although he did note that they could be ruthless and inflict great harm when provoked, they nonetheless kept their word. It is therefore highly probable that we can take bin Laden and the Taliban on their word.

Revolutionary Catechism, a book cited earlier, is rather fascinating because of some of the advice it offers. For example, the authors said that in order to produce

"merciless" destruction, the revolutionary must infiltrate various entities such as the

secret police, the military, the world of business, and, of course, the bureaucracy. They

also divided society into six categories. One of those six involved the more vocal

of the intelligentsia, whom they regarded as problematic and dangerous to the

revolution. For this reason, the book's authors advised that this group was to be

terminated first, the thinking being that their violent deaths would gain wide attention

and cause fear among the government entities.

Another category involved rich and powerful people. The authors referred to

these individuals as "animals", and exhibited little respect for their power or genuine

achievements . The best way to deal with this group, they said, was to blackmail them

or otherwise create serious mischief in their lives. To accomplish the ultimate goals of

the revolution, however, Revolutionary Catechism emphasized the need for the

destruction of the very foundations of Western civilization.

While Revolutionary Catechism is of course indicative of the problems existing in

Russia at the time of its writing, much of the advice it offers appears to have gained

acceptance, at least to some extent, by today's new breed of terrorists. For instance,

during the 1972 Olympic Games in Munich, it is said that members of the Black

September, a radical Palestinian terrorist group, reportedly told the head of the

Egyptian Olympic team who was working to negotiate the freedom of the Israelis being held hostage, "Money means nothing to us; our lives mean nothing to us."

When a nation or a group exhibit this type of rage and this type of conviction, they make for a formidable enemy. It therefore seems reasonable that we can expect more domestic terrorist activity. There are measures that can and are being taken to protect the general population as well as our national assets. There are also measures that can be taken by individuals and businesses to protect themselves. The biggest factors, as we shall see, involve education, planning, and decisive action. In the chapters that follow, these will be discussed at length.

PERSONAL AND BUSINESS RISK ANALYSIS

"Discipline is the soul of an army. It makes small numbers formidable;
procures success to the weak, and esteem to all."

- George Washington (1759)

America is at war, but it's certainly unlike any war we have fought before. Phil Coyle, senior advisor at the Center for Defense Information expressed it best when he said "What happened on September 11 was that our own enterprise, our own commerce, our technologies were turned against us. These were our aircraft, our office buildings - which represent our success - and they were turned into weapons against us."

With the exception of the Revolutionary and Civil Wars, we have not experienced violence of this magnitude on domestic soil nor have we seriously expected any as a result of our military actions abroad. White House Press Secretary Ari Fleischer and other governmental representatives have strongly emphasized that American citizens must prepare for more casualties at home and for the realization that the battle against terrorism will not be quickly resolved.

The threat to personal safety as citizens go about their lives, as they travel, go to work, enjoy certain types of entertainment, and pursue their various interests are neither well understood nor clearly defined. What is understood, however, is that

51

we, as Americans, need to re-think how we live.

In an interview with this author following the 1993 bombing of the World Trade Center, Larry Carpenter, president of Investigative Specialists, Inc. of Las Vegas, Nevada, explained that Americans tend to be very complacent. "It's largely a matter of thinking 'Nothing's happened yet, so why worry.' Unfortunately, that's the kind of thinking that can get a person or a corporation into serious trouble."

Operating under the premise that it is better to err on the side of caution, Carpenter emphasized that it's important to closely examine what our personal and business risks might be and immediately address them.

With this in mind, the following personal security lifestyle questionnaire should prove to be helpful. Keep in mind that identifying and acknowledging threats or risks also brings the opportunity to successfully mitigate many of them. Therefore, instead of viewing the questionnaire from a fear-based perspective, it is more helpful to look at it as an empowering tool for resolution.

DETERMING PERSONAL LIFESTYLE RISK

1. Do you live in a densely populated area or in a more rural environment?

2. Do you live close to large manufacturing or chemical plants, utilities, airports, or entertainment/resort centers?

3. Do you live on or very close to a large military base or government research facility?

4.   Do you routinely eat in high profile restaurants or attend large sporting or other types of public entertainment events?

5.   Do you routinely buy produce from a grocery store or do you instead frequent farmers markets and/or road side stands?

6.   Are you a high profile executive or researcher, do you handle classified information, or do you have responsibility for chemicals, biological agents or pharmaceutical agents?

7.   Would you consider your lifestyle as more sedentary or fast paced and stressful?

8.   Does your work or personal business require frequent long distance or foreign travel?

9.   Do you routinely use freeways or cross large bridges in order to travel to work or shopping?

10. Do you routinely use the same route in going to work, to school, or to shopping?

11. Do you routinely come and go from your home at the same time?

12. Do you routinely lock the doors and windows of your home when absent, and do you routinely lock the doors to your vehicle?

13. Is your vehicle routinely parked in a secured garage area or is it left in a carport or other open, unsecured area?

14. Do you live or work in a high rise building having more than nine floors?

15. Do you routinely use large public or corporate parking facilities or garages and, if so, are they patrolled?

16. Are you a health care worker? If so, do you meticulously follow Universal or (infection control) Precautions?

17. In private, do you <u>carefully</u> and routinely wash your hands after being out in the public, after toilet use, and after working in the soil or handling newspapers, mail, or items used by others?

18. Do you wash your hands <u>carefully</u> before food preparation and, if handling meats, afterwards?

19. Have you taken first aid and CPR training recently?

20. Do you keep a first aid kit on hand which is adequate enough to handle emergency situations if rescue personnel are not immediately available?

21. Do you have an adequate supply of any needed prescription medications in the event delivery services were disrupted temporarily?

22. Do you and your family have an emergency plan for evacuating the various parts of your home if there is a fire or other disaster?

23. Have you determined which area of your home is the safest in the event of a nuclear device detonation and what steps you need to take for decontamination?

24. Do you have an adequate supply of batteries for radios and flashlights?

25. Do you hunt or handle wild animals or their fur?

26. How long has it been since you were vaccinated for smallpox or diphtheria?

27. Do you have any serious health issues which may have compromised your immune system?

28. If you have a seriously ill family member requiring oxygen or other life sustaining treatments, do you have an adequate backup supply or small generator?

29. Are you physically able to remove yourself or an injured or disabled family to a location of safety outside your home if it became necessary? If not, do you have a specially designed assistive device to help with this task or have you designated a neighbor or other family member who can do so?

30. Do you have a two week supply of food and water available in the unlikely event services were temporarily disrupted?

31. Do you have important items like a manual can opener and chlorine bleach for water purification?

32. Do you have a supply of candles and matches?

33. Do you have a list posted of emergency numbers and governmental support agencies?

34. If you and your family are separated, do you have a plan for contacting each other in the event of an emergency situation or disaster?

Thackrah stated that the "purpose of threat analysis is to turn any form of a threat into a manageable problem." These questions are not meant to unduly frighten anyone; rather, they are intended to help individuals proactively examine their lifestyles in order to better protect themselves and their families.

In reviewing the questionnaire, it is necessary to consider the terrorist's point of view. If they are going to eradicate the "Great White Satan", how best might they accomplish this?

Historical evidence has shown that terrorists like to get significant media attention. Remember that in Chapter One Libyan leader Moammar Gadafi was quoted as advocating that, in dealing with America, "Acts of terrorism are the answer and they will by more and more violent and spectacular for television purposes around the world." What we have seen in the past is that terrorist do this by hitting places where large numbers of people frequent such as sporting events, concerts, night clubs or other places of leisure. We have also seen that they have frequently engaged in explosive or incendiary activities, but they can obtain the same media attention by doing multiple strikes at smaller sites - an epidemic here, an explosion there and a goodly amount of anthrax or e coli outbreaks along the way. They can, of course, also gain significant attention by engaging in nuclear, biological, and chemical terrorism activities, of which we know they are now capable.

In looking at the questionnaire, consider your lifestyle - all of it - and then think about if from the terrorist's perspective. Later in this and ensuing chapters, we will discuss the questionnaire in more detail and look at a few ways to circumvent these potential problems.

Obviously, businesses, too, need to engage in threat analysis. Although most have policies and procedures already in place regarding emergencies and general security operations, the insidious nature of the terrorist threat now being faced by this country makes it necessary to re-examine and refine them. If you are a company executive, or if you are a private business owner or administrator, the following is an additional risk analysis questionnaire for your security use:

DETERMINING RISK FOR BUSINESSES

1. Is yours a high profile company in terms of specific location or particular product advertising?

2. Is your company involved with the manufacturing or shipping of chemical, radiological, pharmaceutical, military, or agricultural materials or agents?

3. Is your corporation or company involved with the handling or shipping of food or beverage supplies?

4. Are you in the upper management of a large health care facility or provider organization? Are you in upper management of a large rural or

regional hospital or health care facility?

5.   Are you in upper management of a high profile resort or casino?

6.   As a company executive, are you required to do considerable

domestic and foreign travel?

7.   Do you routinely use the same routes to and from work and do you

routinely use the same parking place?

8.   Do you routinely lock your vehicle and keep the windows closed?

9.   How secure is your company parking area or garage? Are there security

personnel who routinely patrol the area and do you know if background

checks been made on the security agency and all of their personnel?

10.   Does a secretary or other entity routinely handle your travel

arrangements?

11.   Who has access to company travel or meeting schedules?

12.   How and by whom are key electronic submissions secured and handled?

13.   In addition to reviewing your company's "Policy and Procedures" manual,

have employees been well trained in security issues?

14.   Are background checks a routine part of your employee pre-hire practice?

15.   Does your company have a front desk sign-in, guest badging or screening

policy?

16.   How are incoming and outgoing shipments and mail handled and by

whom are they handled? How are handlers monitored and by whom?

17. Who provides company security functions and what is their level of expertise? Do you have a Director or Security and does this individual have adequate experience and/or training in risk assessment, emergency and crisis and counter-terrorism tactics? If there is no Director of Security, has an individual been delegated to provide general oversight in this area?

18. Has your company ever had a professional risk assessment evaluation performed by an outside security provider? If so, how long ago? What was the background of the individuals performing the analysis?

19. If deficiencies were found in the above-mentioned analysis, have they been adequately addressed and have the analysis providers been invited back to review and evaluate the corrections?

20. If yours is a major hospital or health care provider, who monitors the access of pharmaceutical and medical device company representatives? Do they have limited access and, if not, are they escorted to "sensitive" areas?

21. Have company policies and procedures been changed to reflect more stringent security measures now being recommended?

22. Does your company provide routine, thorough security, safety and

emergency evacuation training for all employees?

23.   Do your employees clearly understand their role in personal and company security?

24.   Are you, as a business, financially able to weather the possibility of further attacks on this country and its assets and, if not, what do you need to do now to mitigate this possible threat?

In looking at earlier terrorist communication, literature, events and activities, we know that they routinely target businesses when they think it will serve their purposes. What do you have that they might want? Chemicals? Pathogens? Perhaps radiological medical waste? Or how about a high profile researcher?

Since the late1970's, it has become quite evident that terrorists have increasingly gone after "soft" targets such as innocent civilians. After the events of September 11, 2001, we know this all to well. Although they often are able to obtain their goals by hitting large, media worthy sites, they have also used assassination, extortion, and hostage-taking on a regular basis. High profile business executives have, in fact, served them very well. So in effectively determining risk, it's important to see beyond the immediate and look at <u>all</u> possibilities.

The Personal Lifestyle and Business Risk questionnaires are by no means inclusive. They will, however, provide you as an individual or you as an executive the basics you will need in order prepare and protect yourself and your family, as well as your business. Both questionnaires require careful thought.

Consider this fictional but likely scenario: Janice is a working mother with a young son. She has taken a Friday afternoon off in order to prepare for dinner guests coming that evening. She picks Billy up from daycare before going grocery shopping at a large retail market. While looking at produce, she samples several grapes and gives one to her son to enjoy before she purchases them.

After returning home, Janice puts away the groceries, starts a load of soiled laundry in the washer, and fields several telephone calls from telemarketers. Tired, cranky and very hungry by now, Billy begins crying loudly. Janice feeds him a snack and then puts him down in front of the television to watch his favorite cartoon show. No sooner has she done that then a neighbor comes over to borrow some shortening and they end up talking for 30 minutes.

Panic begins to set in.   Janice hurriedly begins preparing the salad and marinating the steaks, hoping to have them finished and herself showered and dressed before her husband and his new business partners arrive for dinner. As celebratory glasses of wine are poured before the meal, she cringes as she realizes that in her haste she forgot to wash her hands after walking into the house and handling the food both for Billy and for the dinner. "Well," she thinks to herself, "it's not the worst thing that could have happened, that's for sure."

Or consider this: Art is a supervisor for a small chemical manufacturing plant.

He has a departmental budget to review and turn in and a report to complete before

the end of the day. After having been quite late in submitting the two previous reports,

Art knows that if it happens again, he will likely face disciplinary action. Stress is

catching up with him and he has a pounding headache. One of his employees sticks his

head in Art's office and says "Hey Art, we're showing a case missing from the shipment

room. What do you want us to do?"

Indignant at the interruption and the fact that this long-time employee doesn't

seem to have remembered to use the "Policy and Procedure" manual, Art tells him to

check the product holding area and if they can't find the missing case to note the

discrepancy in the log book. "It's no big emergency," he says in obvious exasperation.

"We'll deal with it later, okay!"

And what about this: A well-known company doing government contract work

has strict security procedures and guidelines in place for all employees to follow. A

card entry system is in effect, as well as very specific policies covering admittance.

Late one afternoon, an unknown man pounds on a glass entry door until a passing

employee reluctantly opens it. "I'm with building maintenance," the fellow says, his

standard overalls, badge and clipboard confirming that fact. "I accidently left my card in

the car. I just want to get in to do a quick site survey to see if there was any interior rain

damage from last week. Could you let me in?"

The man is admitted. No attempt is made later to discern if he is indeed with the maintenance department. Instead, he gains easy access and is left on his own.

What do these three scenarios have in common? Each illustrates the ease with which attempted acts of chemical, biological or other form of terrorism can, through our own negligence or lack of awareness, be successfully completed.

A September 1989 Security Management article by Al Foster stressed that "When confronted with an individual who appears to be on a bona fide mission (in a uniform or business suit, carrying a briefcase, clipboard, or toolbox), employees tend to believe the person is there to do a job and they should not interfere. Most times, a strong corporate visitor control program will nip this kind of penetration in the bud, but often, if the attempt is timed right, access can be gained merely by being convincing in the role."

Jan Reber and Paul Shaw, in their book the Executive Protection Manual, pointed out that for terrorists to be successful they need specific information regarding building plans, organizational and corporate activities, security procedures, the location of all personnel, key employee schedules, and the movement patterns, habits, and general lifestyles of top executives and their families. The authors explained that this is accomplished through surveillance, as well as through unauthorized access to homes, offices, telephone conversations, and computer files. The sophisticated technology now commercially available obviously enhances this effort.

The assassination or hostage-taking of key executives of high profile businesses, particularly the multi-nationals with headquarters in this country, is a distinct possibility and well worth our attention. As we saw with Alfred Herrhausen, the head of the Deutsch Bank, in Germany, terrorists were able to use such tactics to gain enormous world media attention and create an atmosphere of fear and panic.

It's important, then, to look carefully at our lifestyle and look very closely at our environment. In performing their surveillance and in preparing for an attack, we know that terrorists often inadvertently provide clues of their forthcoming activity. These are called "pre-incident" indicators. Unfortunately, they can easily be misinterpreted or ignored.

Carl Sifakis, in his Encyclopedia of Assassinations, explained that "In the late 1980's antiterrorist precautions had become a way of life for board members or large West German companies. Most executives traveled in cars equipped with armor plating and bulletproof glass and had drivers trained in antiterrorist tactics." Yet prior to the fatal attack on Herrhausen, mentioned in the first chapter of this book, Red Army Faction members posed as construction workers and were able to work less than 500 yards from Herrhausen's home unnoticed.

What is particularly troubling is that no one living in the fashionable neighbor-hood bothered to check with the city to see if the apparent road work being done was legitimate. As a result, the terrorists were allowed to complete their surveillance activities and eventually place the bomb completely unhampered.

In fact, after establishing what they considered to be the most effective method for the assassination on Herrhausen, the terrorists began making a concerted effort to make the expensive bicycle under which the bomb was placed, blend in with the environment - weeks before the actual incident. Curiously, the bike was left by the side of the road. It was removed and replaced several times, but no one questioned its being there even though a bike rack was very close by.

Had the pre-incident indicators been observed, had surveillance detection been employed, it is quite probable that Herrhausen would be alive today.

In reviewing the scenarios provided in this chapter, consider the first two from the perspective of a chemical and bio-terrorism event. Pathogens, as you may recall, can often be dispersed using aerosol sprays or other means. Earlier, in the first example given, a simple lapse in protocol like that experienced by Janice in giving her son unwashed produce off the store shelf or in forgetting to wash properly before handling food could very easily have produced catastrophic results.

Likewise, ignoring or delaying to report the disappearance of a case of chemicals to the proper authorities could ultimately mean the loss of many lives. However, a simple telephone call, if made by either Art or his employee, could very well prevent such a problem from occurring. As we have seen, terrorists often resort to illegally buying or stealing radioactive, pathogenic or chemical materials with the intent of using them for mass destruction activities like that seen in the Oklahoma City federal building bombing in 1995.

In the last scenario provided, it is evident that even if a company or business has a comprehensive and well-conceived security program with definitive policies and procedures in place, unless employees understand and follow them, they are of very little value. This is equally true for an individual or family.

Some experts feel that Americans have a human characteristic working against them and that is the fact that most of them are creatures of habit and prefer to have an established routine. Moreover, they find that these habits and routines are often difficult to change. But failure to do so can sometimes be detrimental to their health and welfare.

William Buckley, the CIA station chief in Beirut, was taken hostage in 1984 and was later tortured and killed. Despite the fact that he was an intelligence expert educated in terrorism tactics, he apparently refused to vary the route he traveled to work, thereby setting himself up for disaster. With such predictability, he unfortunately allowed himself to be an easy target.

While most of us are not CIA station chiefs and are therefore not facing such a risks, some of the habits we have developed can result in equally disturbing problems. Increased self-discipline, increased awareness and the continual observation of our surroundings are therefore very important protective skills we need to develop.

Reber and Shaw made the following observation that applies as much to individuals as it does to business entities: "A security program can never be based merely upon a response to a specific level of threat. The security program must be an ongoing, positive response to existing problems and potential emergencies...A level of security must be maintained so that all contingencies can be coped with easily."

In September 1993, a bomb scare at the Sparks Nugget Hotel and Casino in Nevada stunned the city and meant a substantial loss of revenue, not only for the property concerned, but also to the businesses in the surrounding areas. While the bomb turned out to be a hoax, its realistic appearance and design made authorities shudder. Further, the fact that someone was able to walk into a busy, well-populated environment and plant a device in a ceiling beam without being detected was also alarming. Certainly law enforcement officials had seen other extortion attempts and bomb scares over the years. Yet the precision and sophistication with which this one was carried out did raise some new and serious risk assessment concerns, which the Nugget's management immediately worked to correct.

Let's take a look at one last scenario: A man is sitting in a crowded airline boarding area. After reading his newspaper for a short time, he abruptly jumps up from his seat and departs from the area leaving his briefcase. He returns in a few minutes with a cup of coffee and resumes reading. After a short time, the man again leaves his seat and does not take the briefcase with him. Ten minutes go by and the owner is nowhere in sight. An observant and concerned by-stander reports the suspicious activity to the counter agent. Security is called and the bag is removed for examination. A hard-to-detect "plastic" bomb is found inside. The simple act of informing the counter agent thwarted a major disaster.

Whether the motivation is political, religious, cultural, or ethnic, terrorists want us to think that they are invincible. They want to create paralyzing fear that will impede the freedoms, movement and financial success of our highly mobile society. As we have seen, they generally plan their operations meticulously to ensure that the element of surprise and drama help them accomplish their goals successfully. But more often than not, they need an unsuspecting public to help them in these efforts.

OUR GOVERNMENT'S ROLE IN PROTECTION

"The condition upon which God hath given liberty to man
is eternal vigilance"

- John Philpot Curran

America's vulnerability in light of current military action in Afghanistan and elsewhere, has raised legitimate concerns that must of course be acknowledged. What happens, people ask, if there is a biological, chemical, or nuclear attack by the terrorists? And what happens if there is a cyber attack and banking and other services are effected? Can we depend on our government to take care of us? How can we help ourselves, our families, our businesses? What are we supposed to do?

Before getting to that, it is well worth mentioning that because of the excellent intelligence gathering by the FBI, CIA, and local law enforcement agencies, America was spared a significant loss of life - not just once, but on a number of previous occasions.

Take, for example, the July 5, 1993 Time magazine article which stated, "The visions were apocalyptic: bomb blasts spreading fire and smoke through United Nations headquarters and a lower Manhattan skyscraper that houses, of all things, the New York offices of the FBI. Other explosions the same day in the Holland and Lincoln tunnels under the Hudson River, crushing motorists inside cars turned to twisted junk, killing many more by spreading intense heat, smoke and noxious fumes throughout the enclosed space of the tubes. Thousands dead, thousands more injured, the nation's biggest city in a wild panic."

Armageddon? Perhaps, but in fact this was part of an aborted plan by a Muslim fundamentalist terrorist group. Thankfully, a SWAT team of FBI agents and New York City police were able to contain it. Had the group succeeded, considerable devastation would have occurred.

According to the Time article, "the team "burst into a garage in the borough of Queens at 1:30 last Thursday morning catching five men hunched over 55-gal. barrels, swirling wood spoons to mix fertilizer and diesel fuel into an explosive paste. The alleged bomb makers were hauled into court, some still wearing overalls splotched with what the local FBI called a 'witches brew'. They and three others nabbed in raids on apartments, all described as Muslim fundamentalists, were charged with conspiracy to carry out the bombings and held without bail."

It must be remembered that in the 1993 World Trade Center bombings, cyanide had been a part of the scenario, the intent being that a much greater degree of damage would be inflicted through its use. The heat that resulted from the explosion was so intense, the cyanide was rendered harmless, thus sparing many lives.

Time reported that "The World Trade Center bombers, for all their ineptitude -

one expert likens them to the Three Stooges - did set off a blast that killed six people and injured more than 1,000. Their would-be imitators failed mostly because a confidential informant inside the ring helped the FBI keep his comrades under close surveillance. FBI men dubbed him 'the Colonel'; he was later identified as Emad Salen, 43, a former Egyptian military officer."

In its October 2, 2001 edition, The National Enquirer reported that in 1998, covert actions by the CIA led to an arrest "that stopped the purchase of nuclear materials that would have given bin Laden the ability to use them in the attacks against the United States!"

The Enquirer stated that the big break for intelligence agents came when the FBI was able to "turn" a former Sudanese aide of bin Laden. This occurred in 1996. They reported "The defector detailed for the U.S. his negotiations to buy $1.5 million worth of uranium for bin Laden in Khartoum, Sudan.'

"During his negotiations, he had a meeting in the town of Bait al-Mal, north of Khartoum. At that meeting, Alfadl was shown a cylinder between two and three feet tall containing uranium, he told FBI agents."

It is said that Alfadl was considered so valuable an asset, the U.S. government has spent nearly one million dollars to protect him since his conversion.

Experts say that the most likely and accessible nuclear device for a terrorist would be the radiological dispersal bomb or "dirty bomb", as it is often called, which can

71

be made by combining high explosives with radioactive materials that are fairly easy to obtain.

Dr. Bruce G. Blair, president of the Center for Defense Information, in an updated October 1, 2001 report, explained that "Massive quantities of fissionable material exist around the world."

Russia, in particular, is known to have very poor security for nuclear waste. Pakistan, India, China, Iran, Iraq and Syria possess nuclear weapons or have nuclear materials. Terrorists, with expertise available from a rogue scientist, could conceivably fabricate a crude nuclear device assuming they were able to obtain the component materials. The countries just mentioned are also known to have arsenals of chemical and biological warfare agents which could be added to the terrorist "bag of tricks".

Recognizing the potential for a terrorist attack in this country, the Federal Emergency Management Agency, the FBI and five other federal agencies developed and published a plan for responding to a domestic threat or incident. Titled the" U.S. Government Interagency Domestic Terrorism Concept of Operations Plan", the document established definitive guidelines for assessing and monitoring a threat, notifying the appropriate agencies, and how resources are to be coordinated and managed to cope with the crisis.

The Departments of Justice, Defense, Energy, Health and Human Services, and the Environmental Protection Agency all participated in the plan's creation, which was the result of a Presidential directive issued in 1995. Although somewhat lengthy, the

Plan is worth mentioning here because it provides a better understanding of how the

federal government responds to terrorist incidents or attacks and how they interact with

state and local entities at such times. In other words, it provides a clear look at what we

can expect from them in dealing with terrorism.

Basically, the Plan states that federal response to a terrorist threat or incident

will be executed under two broad responsibilities: Crisis Management and

Consequence Management. According to the Plan, the Attorney General is

responsible for ensuring the development and implementation of policies directed at

preventing terrorist attacks domestically. The Department of Justice, it states, "has

charged the FBI with execution of its LFA responsibilities for the management of a

Federal response to terrorist threats or incidents that take place within U.S. territory or

those occurring in international waters that do not involve the flag vessel of a foreign

country."

As the Lead Federal Agency (LFA) for crisis management, the FBI designates a

federal On-Scene Commander for the overall coordination between the federal, state,

and local authorities until such time that the Attorney General transfers the LFA role to

the Federal Emergency Management Agency (FEMA).

"As the LFA for consequence management", the Plan says, " FEMA will manage

and coordinate response in support of State and local governments in accordance with its statutory authorities."

In this role, FEMA designates the appropriate liaison and advisory personnel for the FBI's Strategic Information and Operations Center (SIOC) and deployment with the Domestic Emergency Support Team (DEST), and the Joint Information Center.

The Plan explains that "The Department of Defense serves as a support agency to the FBI for crisis management functions, including technical operations and a support agency to FEMA for consequence management." Threat assessment, DEST participation, and the transportation of a weapons of mass destruction device (WMP) are among its responsibilities.

The Department of Energy (DOE) also serves as a support agency to the FBI for technical operations and as a support agency to FEMA for consequence management. In the event of a nuclear/radiological incident or attack, the DOE provides scientific and technical personnel and equipment in support of the lead federal agency.

According to the Plan, "DOE assistance can support both crisis and consequence management activities with capabilities such as threat assessment, DEST deployment, LFA advisory requirements, technical advice, forecast modeling predictions, and operational support to include direct support of tactical operations. Deployable DOE scientific technical assistance and support includes capabilities such as search operations; access operations; diagnostic and device assessment; radiological assessment and monitoring; identification of material; development of

Federal protective action recommendations; provision of information on the radiological

response; render safe operations; hazards assessment; containment; relocation and

storage of special nuclear material evidence; post-incident clean-up; and on-site

management and radiological assessment to the public, the White House, and

members of Congress and foreign governments. All DOE support to a Federal

response will be coordinated through a Senior Energy Official."

The Environmental Protection Agency (EPA) serves in a similar support capacity

to the FBI, providing technical personnel and supporting equipment to the LFA during

all aspects of a WMD terrorist attack. Per the Plan, "EPA assistance may include threat

assessment, DEST and regional emergency response team deployment, LFA advisory

requirements, technical advice and operational support for chemical, biological, and

radiological releases. EPA assistance and advice includes threat assessment,

consultation, agent identification, hazard detection and reduction, environmental

monitoring; sample and forensic evidence collection/analysis; identification of

contaminants; feasibility assessment and clean-up; and on-site safety, protection,

decontamination, and restoration activities."

Under the National Oil and Hazardous Substances Pollution Contingency Plan,

the EPA would work with the United States Coast Guard in the event of oil discharges

into navigable waters or the release of hazardous substances or contaminants into the

environment.

In addition to these agencies, the Department of Health and Human Services (HHS) serves in a support capacity to the FBI for technical operations and as a support agency to FEMA for consequence management. They also provide technical personnel and supporting equipment to the LFA during all aspects of a terrorist incident.

For example, the HHS can provide regulatory follow-up when an incident involves a product regulated by the Food and Drug Administration. The HHS can also provide epidemiological investigation (such as in anthrax cases), and technical advice. Their technical assistance to the FBI may include identification of pathogenic agents, sample collection and analysis, on-site safety and protection activities, and medical management planning.

The HHS operational support to FEMA may include mass immunization, mass prophylaxis, mass fatality management, pharmaceutical support operations (National Pharmaceutical Stockpile), patient tracking and evacuation and medical care provided through the National Disaster Medical System.

This country's laws assign primary authority to the Federal government to prevent and respond to threats or acts of terrorism; however, they assign primary authority to the State and local governments to respond to the consequences of terrorism; the Federal government then provides assistance as required.

Prior to the creation of the Plan, the FEMA had developed what it called The Federal Response Plan (FRP) which outlined how the U.S. government would implement the Robert T. Stafford Disaster Relief and Emergency Assistance Act to assist state and local governments in the event of a major disaster or emergency that would overwhelm "their ability to respond effectively to save lives; protect public health, safety, and property; and restore their communities."

In the Plan's "Foreward", former FEMA Director James Witt explained that the FRP "described the policies, planning assumptions, concept of operations, response and recovery actions, and responsibilities of 27 Federal departments and agencies, including the American Red Cross, that guide Federal operations following Presidential declaration of a major disaster or emergency."

Following the September 11, 2001 attacks, President Bush named former Pennsylvania governor Tom Ridge as head of the newly established Office of Homeland Security, a Cabinet level position. Through an executive order, the president instructed Ridge to work with federal, state and local agencies in the creation of a plan "to detect, prepare for, prevent, protect against, respond to and recover fro terrorists attacks within the United States."

According to an October 8, 2001 Associated Press article, Ridge was tasked with these mandates:

- Set priorities for spying overseas and make sure intelligence agencies have the necessary resources needed

- Develop a biological and chemical release detection system and the means to adequately contain the spread of these agents

- Review hospital capacity and supplies of vaccines and pharmaceuticals

- Fortify security for power plants, communication systems, transportation systems, shipping ports and food and water supplies

The article stated further that "Ridge will set the agenda for a new Homeland Security Council – a domestic version of the National Security Council - that includes the secretaries of Treasury, Defense, Transportation, and Health and Human Services; and the directors of the CIA, FBI and Federal Emergency Management Agency."

Specifically how the U.S. Government Interagency Domestic Terrorism Concept of Operations Plan and the FRP will integrate with the Office of Homeland Security is, at this time, somewhat unclear. It is evident, however, that considerable planning has taken place, both before and after the events of September 11, 2001.

State and local organizations have also been involved in emergency preparedness planning and most participate in emergency drills or exercises on a routine basis. In fact, the Department of Justice has for some time been sponsoring courses in responding to assaults from Weapons of Mass Destruction for first responders such as fire fighters and police officers. Courses to support emergency response to terrorism include: Responder Operations, Radiation and Nuclear Agents, and Incident Command. Among the topics contained in the Responder Operations course is highly detailed training for responding to chemical and biological assaults.

Richard Cole, in an Associated Press article regarding terrorism dated May 27, 1997, mentioned that "The military has improved technology to detect the threats. Experts are training emergency personnel to prevent deaths. The FBI's counter-terrorist staff has been beefed up. Congress has enacted laws to crack down on visas and finances.'

"But there are no easy technological fixes. And the legal solutions almost inevitably run up against the Constitution and the core values of a society that treasures its freedoms."

Cole reported, however, that "Last month, the Pentagon launched the $46.5 million Chem-Bio Quick Response Force aimed at training police, doctors, and fire officials in 120 cities to react to attacks by weapons of mass destruction."

Since 1997, when Cole's article was written, a considerable amount of effort has been placed on emergency preparedness and terrorism.

Clearly, even with such comprehensive planning in place by governmental agencies and organizations, security and emergency planning on the part of private citizens and business entities is still highly advisable. Using the questionnaires provided in the last chapter as a starting point, protective action plans can be easily established.

HOW DO WE PROTECT OURSELVES?

"Protection and patriotism are reciprocal"

John C. Calhoun (1811)

Having earlier reviewed the personal and business-oriented threat analysis questionnaires, the obvious question is "What now?" How do we use that analysis to protect ourselves?

The answer to this lies in the creation of a Personal Security Plan that identifies possible areas where we feel we may be the most vulnerable, and then concretely defines solutions we believe to be most appropriate and practical for our particular lifestyle.

While some individuals may feel that a written plan is of little value, in reality most of us are better served by having a definitive written document that we can refer to from time to time. Additionally, a written plan often generates more immediate action.

Regardless of whether we are discussing personal or business-related security issues, having a definitive plan and then sticking to it is important. Moreover, knowing that you have taken the necessary steps to ensure your protection and that of your family and business is empowering and provides an increased sense of peace and confidence.

A Personal Security Plan may take any form you prefer. It can be an elaborate, multi-paged document or much more simple. It could even take the form of a checklist. In any case, the important thing is that it definitively identifies the potential problem areas, well as the intended solutions. Ideally, the plan should also provide solutions that will address more than one possible scenario.

If, for example, you live in a high risk area such as an apartment building adjacent to a large, high profile financial center, one part of your plan might be to establish a network with neighbors to provide surveillance detection activities (or at least an increased awareness of your surroundings in the event of pre-incident indicators). Signing up for First Aid and CPR training might be another, as might ensuring that you have a two-week supply of food in the event distribution service was temporarily disrupted.

If you have ill or disabled family members, your plan might include holding a family emergency evacuation drill to determine the best strategies for dealing with their condition. If oxygen, ventilator or other equipment or medical supplies are being used, the plan might call for the purchase of a small generator in the event power was temporarily disrupted or the stockpiling of additional supplies in the event delivery systems were temporarily disrupted.

A business owner or executive, might decide that additional front desk or admissions policies need to be rewritten. One issue often needing consideration is the corporate perception of threat and how that is communicated to employees. For this reason, your plan might include employee education. Or perhaps your shipping and receiving departments need to have increased security measures implemented.

Foster, cited earlier, recommends that businesses establish an ongoing program of security, test and evaluation, or ST&E.

ST&E is not new and is, in fact, a concept that has frequently been used by the military. Basically, it takes a look at the effectiveness of existing security operations. Using a "tiger team" approach, highly trained players try to penetrate or breach computer systems, as well as security and protective devices.

While the hiring or training of such teams is expensive and seldom done in civilian settings, Foster said that business owners and executives can nonetheless greatly enhance the effectiveness of their security systems by looking at them from the point of view of a burglar or terrorist, maintaining that it is better to find the holes and plug them yourself before they can be breached or exploited by nefarious intruders.

To illustrate the types of discoveries that can be made, Foster reported "During my late night testing, I contrived to use crude tools consisting of a yardstick with a two-inch nail imbedded in the end and a cheap butane lighter. I heated the nail and quickly slid the yardstick under the door as far as it would go. I slowly moved it around until the sensor on the inside ceiling found the warmth. With automated efficiency, the system immediately unlocked the door. I was admitted into our sanctum sanctorum with the willing assistance of the very systems that were supposed to keep the bad guys out."

Foster emphasized that we must "Cultivate the habit of looking at every entrance, every window and crawlspace, every communications conduit and electrical power feedline, and ask yourself, 'What would it take to get through there, disrupt communication lines, or disable power?"

In attempting to protect themselves, some businesses as well as many private homeowners rely on the services of security agencies. While there are definite benefits, such as possible crime deterence, it's important to keep in mind that the background, training, and experience level of their personnel may vary considerably. For example, some of these individuals get their start in Loss Prevention or have no former security background at all. Even if some have had a law enforcement background, their training and experience may be more heavily geared toward response rather than surveillance detection and incident prevention. Of even greater concern is the fact that adequate background checks are not always performed on these personnel prior to their being hired.

One business hired a night security officer to patrol its property, but discontinued the service when it was found that the man routinely slept on the job and was falsifying his reports regarding the performance of his nightly rounds. It was later found that he had been fired from a previous service for the same behavior.

Using a security agency is not without value and, in fact, is a good idea. The key is to ensure that agency personnel have the experience and training to provide the specific type of security protection you require.

Let's look at some other likely problem scenarios and possible solutions that might be implemented in a Personal Security Plan.

For example, let's say you work for a high profile financial agency that is housed in a prominent multi-storied building. The parking garage has a security patrolman on duty during the day, so you seldom lock your car. One problem you identify is that someone could easily use your unlocked vehicle as a place from which to detonate an explosive device. You would note the problem and the solution -"Keep vehicle locked."

You also identify a problem with the fact that your office is on the 14th floor of the building and contains a maze of cubicles. In the event of a disaster, navigating through them might be difficult. The solution you note is that " The fastest route to Exit One is by going through the marketing area, but there are big windows that might mean a lot of glass shards. Exit two is a farther distance away but may possibly be safer. The easiest access to it is to cut through human resources."

Or let's say you have children and are concerned about their safety in the event of an emergency situation occurring while they are at home, particularly during the period after school before you come home from work. One possible solution you identify is that you will hold evacuation drills so that each family member knows the best

85

ways to escape from different parts of the house. The second is that you will enroll the

oldest, a teenager, in First Aid and CPR training and, last, a list of emergency numbers

will be kept next to both telephones in the house in the event the children should need

them.

Perhaps instead you are an executive of a small, but fairly high profile company.

You see some security issues. They've been brought up before but ignored. In looking

at your plan you think about the fact that, in addition to your own personal security,

everyone in the building is potentially at risk because of security lapses. You decide on

a two-fold solution: You will talk with upper management again about your concerns

and you will also enact your own departmental security and emergency education

program. In this way, you will at least be assured that your department is prepared.

The Red Cross and other experts suggest that, to the degree that is possible and

appropriate, you include all family members in the planning process so they more fully

understand the importance of preparation and teamwork. If you are single, you may

want to create a plan with a trusted neighbor or friend because the saying "two heads

are better than one" is particularly true during the solution ideas creation stage.

Initially such planning may seem like a ridiculous exercise, but keep in mind

that governments and even terrorists routinely spend considerable time in this

endeavor. In fact, once you begin to identify potential security problems and explore

possible solutions, you will find that your awareness and observation skills will begin to increase significantly. Moreover, the very dynamics involved tend to elicit more

positive and effective solutions.

Winston Churchill's remark that "The only thing we have to fear is fear itself"

is certainly applicable when it comes to the challenges America is now facing.

Once we are armed with a plan that identifies the issues, as well the concrete

solutions, we are able to take control of the situation even though there may still be

some unknowns. Fear then becomes an ally, not a foe. Further, the desire of the

terrorists to undermine our resolve is lessened considerably.

PERSONAL SECURITY: THE CHOICE IS OURS

"We are not weak if we make a proper use of
those means which the God of Nature has placed
in our power...The battle, sir, is not to the strong,
it is to the vigilant, the active, the brave."

- Patrick Henry (1775)

What will be the next terrorist attack? According to the U.S. Department of

Justice Radiation and Nuclear Agents Course manual, "This, unfortunately is an

unanswerable question. Where a terrorist will attack is likely to occur, or what types of

weapons will be used, can never be answered with certainty. We can prepare for

generalities, but will never be able to predict when, where, or how a terrorist will attack

us. The best we can do is be prepared, and respond in a timely, efficient manner when

it happens."

Clearly, with the personal safety issues we face today, identifying potential risks

by using the questionnaires provided earlier and by formulating solutions through the

creation of a definitive plan are important first steps. In order to move beyond that,

however, it's vital that we now look at specific actions that will need to be taken in the

event certain emergency situations arise.

What, for example, do we do if there is a suspected problem involving the contamination of our water supply or if there is a nuclear attack of some sort? What if there is an explosive device detonated at a chemical manufacturing plant that results in widespread contamination? What action would we need to take?

First, the compilation of a "**Survival Kit**" should be an immediate priority. Its contents will need to include the following:

- A well-stocked First Aid kit (don't forget to include scissors and tweezers)

- Chlorine bleach for water purification (or water purification tablets)

- An ABC fire extinguisher

- A crescent wrench and pipe wrenches to turn off utilities if necessary

- Emergency supplies of non-perishable food and water (one gallon per person per day). If you have pets, additional water and food for them should be included. Remember that plastic water containers are preferable because they don't break easily.

- A shovel and pick axe, as well as a knife and heavy duty hammer

- A portable battery operated radio and extra batteries

- Several flashlights and extra batteries and bulbs

- A supply of candles and matches

- Large plastic trash bags

- Heavy tape for sealing windows and doors in the event of a nuclear emergency or accident

90

- Extra blankets

- A "backup" supply of prescription medicines, prescription eyeglasses, feminine hygiene supplies (if appropriate), soap, tooth paste, and toilet paper

- State map

- Camping and outdoor survival equipment in the event leaving your home became necessary or if portions of your home were to sustain damage.

- Important family records and an inventory of household items (for insurance purposes)

Some survival experts suggest keeping a supply of cash on hand in the event immediate evacuation is necessary. Additionally, they also suggest having an emergency medical book, road flares, plastic tubing for siphoning gasoline, rope, and a back-packer's cooking stove and fuel included in the survival kit. Other experts add that multiple vitamins, and a supply of energy food bars are also a good idea.

Is this paranoia? Definitely not. The American Red Cross has long suggested that individuals and families keep extra food and survival necessities on hand in the event of natural disasters or other emergency situations. A minimum of a two-week's supply of food seems prudent in the event of a temporary disruption in retail delivery services. However, some survivalist publications suggest keeping as much as a six-month supply and, in fact, members of the Mormon faith are instructed to keep a year's worth of food on hand for general emergency purposes. The term "Mormon Closet" refers to this storage.

When purchasing non-perishable foods and juices, buy what you can reasonably expect to use if no emergency situation arises. Use a rotational system: Date it with a waterproof pen or marker and use the oldest first. In this way, you will not experience waste and will always have fresh, high quality food available when it is needed.

Ideally, survival kit items should be kept in large plastic or vinyl storage container and housed in a protected location such as a closet or pantry. It is helpful to tape a list of the contents of each container on its lid for easier access.

While putting together a Survival Kit is an immediate priority, it is also important to become familiar with general emergency preparedness information, as well as the actions you will need to take if specific types of terrorist events or incidents occur.

Since they are a source of great public worry, let's look at **Weapons of Mass Destruction** (or WMD) first so we have a fuller understanding of the issues involved. The FBI categorizes WMD's into five categories: Nuclear, Chemical, Biological, Incendiaries, and Explosives.

According to the highly informative United States Department of Justice "Responder Operations Course" manual defines a WMD (Title 18, USC 2332a) as "Any explosive, incendiary, bomb, grenade, rocket having a propellant charge of more than four ounces, missile having and explosive or incendiary charge of more than one-quarter pound, mine, or any device similar to the above mentioned. Any device containing a poison gas, any weapon involving a disease organism, or any weapon designed to release radiation or radioactivity at a level dangerous to human life."

The manual states further that some of these devices can range from a simple pipe bomb to a vehicle equipped with an explosive device. For instance, two pounds of Semtex were detonated aboard Pan Am Flight 103 over Lockerbie Scotland, which caused 270 deaths. Although the amount of explosives in the device was fairly small, it was still considered to be a WMD under the definitions of the Federal government.

When detonated, the manual explains, "explosives produce three primary effects: blast pressure, fragmentation, and thermal effects. A fourth effect, ground or seismic shock, is possible, but will normally only be generated by large detonations such as the Oklahoma City bombing which registered on seismic equipment hundreds of miles from the scene."

As we know, explosives can cause significant collateral damage and, if they include nuclear or chemical materials or agents, they can wreak considerably more havoc.

The type and amount of the explosives used, as well as their placement, are of course, important factors. In the February 1993 World Trade Center bombing, a truck filled with 1,200 pounds of Urea Nitrate was used along with an explosive device. That attack killed 6 people, but injured more than 1,000.

93

One type of terrorist weapon worth noting is the "breaking device" in which a chemical or biological agent is encapsulated. When broken, the agent is released to the unsuspecting targets. The device is of particular interest because it can take the form of a light bulb, balloon, or even a thermos bottle. While it tends to be more limited in terms of the dissemination and downwind hazard to unprotected individuals, it is nonetheless a concern.

As we have seen, mechanical spraying devices are quite effective for dispersing biological and chemical agents and can certainly create very unpleasant results. Aerosol cans, crop dusting aircraft and even the exhaust systems of automobiles have been used for this purpose. Interestingly, though, in the case of the Aum Shinrikyo perpetrated subway attack in Tokyo, simple bags of Sarin were placed in subway tunnels. They were punctured with umbrella tips and the airflow from passing trains then successfully carried the toxin through the tunnels.

We know that the use of improvised nuclear devices by terrorists is a growing concern, as is the possible use of a conventional nuclear weapon. Nuclear, biological, and chemical issues and protective guidelines will be more concretely addressed later in this chapter.

In the meantime, it is worth mentioning that experts continue to emphasize the great importance of being alert at all times not only for pre-incident indicators, but also for actual devices that might be surreptitiously placed by terrorist operatives.

The Responder Operations Course manual lists these warning signs that require great caution and need to be immediately reported to authorities:

- Any abandoned container which is out of place for the surroundings

- Obvious devices or containers having blasting caps, timers, booster charges and so forth.

- Abandoned vehicles not clearly belonging in the immediate environment

- Strong chemical odors with no apparent source

- Unusual or foreign devices attached to pressurized containers, bulk storage containers, and supply pipes

- Trip wires or other booby traps, such as suspicious mailing containers

- The receipt of a written or verbal threat

If any of these warning signs are observed, do not attempt to handle, cover, or move the item in question. Also, move upwind from its location and call local law enforcement authorities to report the finding. If the suspected device is in a building or other enclosure, and it is possible to do so, try to shut doors and windows as you leave to isolate the release of any harmful agents in the event that detonation may occur.

In the case of the receipt of a written or verbal threat or suspicious mail, it's equally as important to contact the FBI or law enforcement officials. Recently reported anthrax cases were often preceded by the receipt of suspicious mail. Should you ever receive a letter or package that has excessive postage, appears to be soiled or stained, contains powder, or otherwise causes concern , the Centers for Disease Control and

Prevention urge that the following precautions be taken:

- Do not shake or empty the contents of the suspicious package.

- Place the package or mail item in a plastic bag or container.

- Leave the room in which the package or mail item is located and close the door.

- Wash hands with soap and water.

- Report the incident to the police.

- Do not clean any powder that has spilled.

Returning to the WMD issue, the importance of understanding the protective

actions that should be taken if certain terrorist-inspired events occur cannot be

emphasized enough. Although general preparedness information will be provided later

in this chapter, it's helpful to examine specific WMD threat possibilities more closely.

NUCLEAR OR RADIOLOGICAL ATTACK

The very word "nuclear" automatically tends to evoke fear in the minds of most

individuals. Yet while they tend to worry about the threat of a major nuclear attack,

some experts feel that the use of a smaller radiological dispersal device - radiological

materials combined with high explosives - is a much more likely scenario. Their

reasoning is that the availability of these component materials is greater, as well as the

fact that their creation does not take the degree of expertise or sophistication necessary for the production of a conventional nuclear weapon.

Federal guidelines base emergency efforts on the projected doses within the affected area. Obviously the closer individuals are to the epicenter or "ground zero", the greater their radiation exposure and related health effects will be.

If a nuclear or radiological incident or accident were to happen, federal emergency response personnel who are experts in areas such as device assessment, device disablement, intelligence analysis, consequence assessment and management and health physics would be deployed. These individuals, along with state and local agencies, would work to mitigate risk and exposure, as well as to perform clean-up activities.

In his article "Surviving a Terrorist Nuke", Duncan Long reported that "The blast wave will create several real dangers. Indoors, glass is the worst worry even some distance from the blast. Closer to ground zero, other flying debris like plaster or chunks of wood become equally dangerous and the blast itself can send YOU flying if you don't have the sense to get down. Consequently, you should dive for cover behind something that will offer protection both from the thermal radiation as well as blast-hurled missiles."

Naturally, protective actions depend on the size and location of the device used. Keep in mind that whether you are at home or elsewhere at the time of a nuclear or radiological attack, it is important to remain indoors to avoid possible contamination. If you have a basement, move to that location or to an area that you feel will provide the most protection.

According to the U.S. Environmental Protection Agency's Manual of Protective Action Guides & Protective Actions for Nuclear Incidents (Doc. #EPA400-R-92-001), the first floor of a wood framed house would offer an exposure reduction of 10%. By being in the basement of that same house, there would be an exposure reduction of 40%. A masonry house, without a basement, would also offer an exposure reduction of 40%. If, however, you are in a large office or industrial building, the exposure reduction rate could be as much as 80%, depending on your particular location within the building and other factors.

If a nuclear or radiation related attack or incident should occur, keep your radio on and follow instructions provided by the Emergency Broadcast Network, as well as by local, state and federal authorities. These entities will advise you as to the steps you will need to take based on your distance from the epicenter, as well as the wind path, particle migration route, evacuation routes, and the location of monitoring and decontamination centers.

Be prepared to evacuate if necessary. If you have an infant or very young children, you will need to take a supply of diapers and formula with you in the event you are delayed in returning to your home. If you or your family members take prescription drugs or require insulin, you will also want to take an adequate supply with you if an evacuation is called. Of course, it's good to take proper identification, credit cards, a supply of cash, and a fresh change of clothes. The American Red Cross advises

taking important family documents and records, as well.

You may hear the following terms used:

- To **Shelter in Place** means to remain where you are (home, office, etc.)

  and to protect yourself by closing all doors and windows and turning off

  fans and air conditioning or heating systems, etc.

- An **Evacuation** is the urgent removal of people from an area in order to

  avoid or reduce high-level, short-term radiation exposure.

- A **Relocation**, on the other hand, is the removal or continued

  exclusion of people from contaminated areas to avoid chronic radiation

  exposure.

- **Re-entry** is the temporary entry into a restricted zone under controlled

  conditions.

- **Recovery** is the process of reducing contaminant concentrations in the

  affected environment and the resulting exposure rates so that levels are

  acceptable for reoccupation or use.

If an evacuation is called, the wearing hats or scarves, long sleeved shirts, pants,

and sturdy boots or shoes will offer the most protection from particulate exposure.

Often when natural disasters have occurred in the past, we have read about individuals who have refused to follow evacuation orders, opting instead to remain in their homes and "weather the storm". In the case of a nuclear or radiological incident or accident, the ramifications are far too serious to even consider doing this.

In the event of a nuclear or radiological incident or attack, those in the immediate "ground zero" area would experience the maximum exposure and would suffer the largest consequences. Those farthest away, although they may still be contaminated, would have the best chances for survival.

Exposure to radioactive materials can be devastating. Victims may suffer severe radiation burns and radiation poisoning. The previously cited Radiation and Nuclear Agents Course manual reports that "Purpura, or bleeding under the skin, is one of the symptoms of acute radiation sickness. In the days and weeks following the Japanese atomic bombings, the heavily exposed survivors experienced fever, nausea, vomiting, lack of appetite, bloody diarrhea, epilation, and purpura or petechia (a round, purplish red spot caused by bleeding under the sin), sores in their throat or mouth (nasopharyngeal ulcers), and decay and ulceration of the gums about the teeth (necrotic gingivitis). The time of onset of these symptoms varied, but generally occurred sooner among the heavily exposed."

The primary radiation exposure pathways for the general public are immersion during plume passage and exposure from radioactive materials deposited on the ground and other surface areas. Other possible sources include the contamination of clothing and skin, the consumption of contaminated food and water, and, of course, the inhalation of re-suspended radioactive materials.

If you are outdoors when a nuclear or radiological attack or incident occurs, immediately seek shelter. Follow instructions provided by the Emergency Broadcast Network or emergency response personnel and proceed to the nearest public monitoring and decontamination center. If you think you may have been contaminated, shower off thoroughly and replace clothing as soon as possible. It is very important to advise emergency response personnel of the possible contamination in the event medical treatment may also be required. Needless to say, medical treatment for a serious injury would always take priority over decontamination.

Depending on the nature and location of the attack, food and water supplies may be effected. Local, state and federal emergency response teams will advise you if this is the case. However, food and water stored in your home that is unopened or covered and away from direct contamination should be safe to consume.

BIOLOGICAL ATTACK

As discussed in Chapter Two, biological weapons are of greater concern because they are relatively inexpensive and they are also easier to acquire or produce than nuclear materials. Too, biological agents are virtually undetectable and may be disseminated through a variety of means. More importantly, the fear that is inspired by this form of terrorism is often enormous.

101

Dr. Jeffrey P. Koplan, M.D., of the Centers for Disease Control and Prevention (CDC) in Atlanta, commented on October 2, 2001 that "With the heightened awareness to potential terrorists in the wake of September 11, the work that we've accomplished during the last three years to prepare for bioterrorism or chemical emergency is being put to the test."

Terrorism experts have acknowledged that bioterrorism is now a reality in this country. Although it was briefly discussed in Chapter Two, let's closely re-examine the diseases that experts see as the most likely to be used as a terrorist weapon.

Until quite recently, **anthrax** cases in the United States were extremely rare. Also called the "Wool Soiters disease", anthrax is an acute infectious disease which attacks the skin, lungs, and gastrointestinal tract. It is caused by the spore-forming bacterium *Bacillus anthracis* and although it is most common in hoofed animals, it can also be spread to humans through exposure to the tissue of an infected animal or by the inhalation of anthrax spores. It is not spread through person-to-person contact, however.

There are two main types of anthrax, cutaneous (skin) and inhalational. The incubation period for cutaneous anthrax is one to seven days. Early symptoms include itching and often lesions on the skin. There will also be nausea, fever, chills, and the swelling of lymph nodes. If untreated, exhaustion, breathing difficulty, and cardiac distress will occur within two to four weeks.

Inhalational anthrax is the most deadly form. Symptoms include coughing, severe breathing problems and shock. Unless victims receive immediate treatment with antibiotics, death will inevitably follow.

If a person is exposed to anthrax, infection can be prevented with antibiotic treatment. Unfortunately, the fear that has arisen from the recent outbreak of anthrax has cause inappropriate antibiotic use in some instances.

Public concern due to the recent increase in reported anthrax cases has placed considerable pressure on health officials who are being overwhelmed with calls and questions about anthrax vaccines, antibiotic use, and similar topics . In fact, consumers are demanding Cipro (ciprofloxacin) and other antibiotics from their physicians for use as a prophylactic against the disease. They are also purchasing these drugs off the Internet.

"Physicians have a tremendous responsibility here,"warned U.S. Surgeon General David Satcher. "If these drugs are used inappropriately, the organism is going to develop resistence to them. The worst thing you can do is contribute to these organisms becoming resistant."

William Hall, President of the American College of Physicians-American Society of Internal Medicine, agreed, saying "To have all of America on a wide-spectrum antibiotic would do more harm than anthrax would do."

Although a vaccine is available, it is not being recommended for the general public at this time.

The **Smallpox** virus is another possible threat we should more fully understand. Caused by the *variola virus*, the incubation period is between seven to seventeen days. It is typically spread by "droplet infection" from sneezing and by direct contact with the victim. The disease can also be spread through the handling of contaminated clothing or bed linens. Some historians believe that during the French and Indian War, the British may have used smallpox against the Native Americans by giving them contaminated blankets from the beds of smallpox victims.

Can smallpox, too, be spread through aerosol dispersal? Definitely.

Early symptoms include fatigue, a high fever, and head and back aches. In two to three days, a rash characteristically appears on the face, arms, and legs. The rash, which eventually spreads to cover the body, starts with flat red spots which turn into raised lesions. In several more days, they become filled with pus. Crusts or scabs begin to form on these in the second week. Once the scabs have disappeared, the victim will no longer be contagious.

Smallpox can sometimes cause blindness caused by scaring the cornea. If the sores spread to the mouth and throat, the victim will be unable to eat or swallow. Further, they can sometimes grow to cause giant hemorrhaging lesions. Although most smallpox victims will recover, death can occur.

Routine vaccination against smallpox was terminated in 1972, as it was thought that the disease had been eliminated. Although the government has the vaccine stockpiled, it is not recommending mass vaccinations at this time.

Sadly, there is no proven treatment for smallpox; however, supportive therapy such as intravenous fluids and the use of systemic analgesics to control pain and fever. Antibiotics may be given for secondary infections that might occur, however.

The **Ebola or Marburg** viruses, which produce hemorrhagic fevers, can infect monkeys and chimpanzees, as well as humans. Usually found in Africa, we know that the disease is spread through blood and other body fluids. The viruses can, of course, also be dispersed by terrorists though aerosol use.

This terrifying disease affects the capillaries in the body and will eventually cause severe bleeding from multiple sites including the lungs, eyes, nose, and other body orifices, as noted previously in Chapter Two. As might be expected, the mortality rate is high.

The incubation period for these viruses is four to sixteen days. Initial symptoms include nausea, loss of appetite and muscle aches, followed by vomiting, sore throat, abdominal pain and diarrhea. Chest pain may also occur. Victims may become apathetic, dehydrated and disoriented.

Currently there is no vaccine or treatment available to counter these viruses, or the highly contagious Soviet created (gene-mutated) **Chimera virus**.

Plague, or the "black death" as it used to be called, is caused by the bacterium

Yersinia pestis. The disease got its name because dried blood forms under the skin, causing it to turn blackish in appearance. It is normally transmitted to humans by rats through infected fleas, but it can also be spread by person-to-person contact and, of course, through terrorist use of an aerosol spray.

As we have seen, there are three types of plague: bubonic, septicemic, and pneumatic. It is the pneumatic plague which can be covertly transmitted through aerosol use as it would be inhaled into the respiratory tract.

After entering the body, **bubonic plague** bacilli rapidly spread through the lymphatic system and causes enlarged lymph nodes in the groin area called buboes. The incubation period for bubonic plague is two to six days. Symptoms typically include fever, chills, headache, the spitting up of blood, and shortness of breath.

If it invades the bloodstream, instead, it causes **septicemic plague,** which produces a generalized infection and may affect the lungs, spleen, spinal cord, and brain. Septicemic plague is often fatal.

Pneumonic plague also spreads rapidly, after an incubation period of two to three days. Treatment with antibiotics is generally successful. If untreated, however, the mortality rate is 90 to 100%.

For all types, the antibiotic used will depend on the location and severity of the disease. A vaccine is available; however, it unfortunately only protects against the bubonic, not the pneumonic plague.

Tularemia is caused by the bacterium *Francisella tularensis* and can affect both humans and animals. It is typically spread through the handling or eating of meat from an infected rabbit or other animal, but is not spread through person-to-person contact. Again, in a terrorist attack, it could be dispersed through the use of an aerosol spray.

Tularemia has an incubation period of three to six days and produces symptoms of sudden on-set fever, chills, headache, generalized muscle aches, and painful joints. Without treatment with antibiotics, tularemia can be fatal.

There is no current vaccine, although one is in the process of being developed.

Another big worry is **Botulism**, a muscle-paralyzing disease caused by a toxin from the bacterium called *Clostridium botulinum*. It poses a more serious threat, perhaps, because it is so easy to produce and the results can be quite lethal.

Botulism is usually spread by eating contaminated food, but could be spread by terrorists through the use of an aerosol spray as well. Food-borne botulism causes symptoms such as double vision or blurred vision, drooping eyelids, slurred speech, difficulty swallowing, muscle weakness that spreads through the body, and dry mouth. These symptoms occur between two to thirty-six hours after ingestion, although they could appear within up to two weeks according to the CDC. If an antitoxin is not provided, paralysis of breathing can occur, causing death.

The CDC maintains a supply of the antitoxin against botulism. In the event of an outbreak, the antitoxin would be immediately shipped to the state or area affected.

In re-examining bioterrorism, it is evident that aerosol sprays are a common denominator in terms of threat potential. Because the diseases listed are among the pathogens terrorists are suspected to now have available to them, individuals who fear they have possibly been exposed to anthrax, smallpox, botulism, plague, or other serious disease need to contact a physician or emergency health care center immediately for proper diagnosis and treatment.

E Coli and **staphylococcus enterotoxin B** are also terrorist possibilities, but they are not considered to be as serious a threat, at least at this time.

The Health Alert Network (HAN), of which the CDC plays a leadership role, is a nationwide program that links local health departments to one another and to other health organizations including hospitals, private laboratories, the CDC, and federal agencies.

According to Dr. Koplan, "The Federal Response Plan, including the Emergency Support Function #8 which engages the Department of Health and Human Services, was activated September 11. CDC is working closely with other federal agencies and involved state and local partners in providing public health assistance where needed.

In terms of protective measures that can be taken against biological attack, medical experts advise increased awareness and vigilance, **strict** adherence to Universal or Standard Precautions regarding infection control (provided earlier in this chapter) and the following of general health recommendations such as getting adequate sleep, exercise and nutrition as the best routes for protection at this time. Also, fruits and vegetables should be purchased from a reliable source and carefully washed before eating or cooking. Additionally, meats should be thoroughly cooked before consumption.

CHEMICAL ATTACK

The availability and relative low cost of chemical agents also makes them a significant concern to authorities. Additionally, they are easy to produce and small quantities can actually cause significant damage.

Chemical agents are typically disseminated as either an aerosol or as a gas. In their liquid form, some will boil at low temperatures and become gases. Skin contamination and inhalation may then occur if there is exposure.

The Responder Operations Course manual points out that "military grade agents that are weaponized" is a military term that means "the purity of the agent is very high and it can be delivered to the target location by means of a weapon system such as artillery, rockets, planes or spray devices. In the WMD world, this means the chemical agent is very pure, and therefore very deadly, and that the terrorist has figured out a way to deliver it to the target."

Indicators might possibly include unusual people in the area, unexplained spraying or the appearance of unexplained spraying devices, strange odors, or the appearance of dead birds and animals. Once again, increased vigilance and the

109

reporting of any unusual activity is vitally important in protecting against terrorism.

Chemical agents are classified as toxic or incapacitating, based on their effects. VX, Sarin, Chlorine, Phosgene, Mustard Gas, and Hydrogen Cyanide are examples of chemical agents.

Nerve agents work by upsetting the nervous system's ability to function. Symptoms for this type of poisoning include dimness of vision and pinpointed pupils, pain around the eyeball or in the frontal area of the head, as well as nausea, chest tightness, and involuntary twitching and convulsions. If no antidote is provided, death will follow.

Mild to moderate skin exposure will produce nausea and vomiting, and muscle twitching. These symptoms usually occur within 10 minutes to 18 hours after contact.

Severe exposure to a nerve agent would produce, in addition to the other symptoms, breathing difficulty or the cessation of breathing, generalized muscle twitching or paralysis and convulsions. There would also be a loss of bowel and bladder control and loss of consciousness. Again, death will occur without the use of an antidote. These symptoms may occur within a few minutes to up to an hour following exposure.

The antidote for a nerve agent victim is a two-shot system consisting of Atropine and Pralidoxime Chloride, along with follow-up medical care. Diazepam, which is an anti-convulsant drug, may also be given by medical personnel to reduce brain damage.

Blister agents, as the name implies, cause cellular damage to the skin resulting in blisters. Initial symptoms may include stinging and redness. These agents can severely damage the skin, eyes, and respiratory system.

While there are no specific medications for blister agent victims, the biggest concern is secondary infection. Medical treatment may include the application of soothing creams or lotions, use of systemic analgesics, use of antibiotics, and other management methods.

Pulmonary or Choking agents such as phosgene and chlorine are among the most easily accessible agents for terrorists. The Responder Operations Course manual indicates that "Phosgene (CG) gas was used extensively during World War I, causing more than 80% of the chemical agent casualties, and is widely used today as an industrial chemical. The good news is that it dissipates quickly and only affects the lungs with a normally short duration of effectiveness. At most, effects last only a few minutes so the only protection required is a mask. There is no specific medication for a choking agent casualty. Self-aid consists of getting out of the contaminated area and masking, if there is a mask available. If symptoms become moderate to severe, it is best to keep the victim in a sitting position. Victims should obey strict bed rest and be administered oxygen and IV fluids. Bronchodilators and antibiotics, when indicated, may also be advised. Decontamination is accomplished by flushing with water."

Blood agents such as Cyanide and Cyanogen Chloride are widely used in electroplating, dyeing, printing, photography, agriculture and the manufacture of paper, textiles, and plastics. Symptoms of blood agent poisoning include flushed skin, reddish lips (blue in dark skinned individuals), headache, weakness, hypertension followed by hypotension and bradycardia (a slowed heart rate), muscular rigidity or convulsive twitching, abdominal pain, frothing at the mouth, vomiting, and unconsciousness. These symptoms will soon be followed by death if no antidote is given immediately.

Medical personnel typically treat blood agent exposure using amyl nitrite or sodium nitrite. Following this, sodium thiosulfate may be administered.

Chemical agent detection and response are not endeavors that should be undertaken by the general public. Any suspected problems or suspicious activity should be immediately reported to authorities so that appropriate steps, including medical treatment of victims, may be rapidly initiated.

Whether nuclear, biological, or chemical materials are used or, instead, explosives or incendiary devices, we know that the threat of terrorism, and the ability to deliver on that threat, is very real. In order to prepare for the possibility of a surprise terrorist attack, the following information will help you:

GENERAL EMERGENCY PREPAREDNESS INFORMATION

- Determine which is the safest area within your home. Ideally, it should have a solid door and few or no windows. A radio and telephone should be kept there, as should a survival kit.

112

- In times of true emergency, we often have to rely on others. Get acquainted with your neighbors and discuss mutual security planning with them. Learn about the various skills and abilities of each.

- In the event of chemical, biological or radioactive material contamination, remove all your clothing and shower off with soap and water as soon as you are able. Immediately contact health authorities for further assistance if that is possible. It goes without saying that contaminated clothing should be carefully handled and discarded to avoid further contamination.

- In the event of a chemical, biological or radioactive materials attack, keep a radio (or television if it is working) turned on for important information from the Emergency Broadcast Network regarding situational updates and evacuation routes if such action becomes necessary.

- Due to health regulations, animals are not allowed inside emergency shelters. If you believe evacuation may occur, place the animals in the safest location possible and provide adequate food and water for them.

- Immediately discard all open food and beverages that might be contaminated.

- Eat perishable foods first. Freezer foods will last anywhere from 48 to 72 hours if the freezer is fairly full and the door is kept closed.

- To treat water, add 10 drops of chlorine bleach to each gallon of water and allow it to stand for 30 minutes before consuming.

- If necessary, emergency water may be taken from toilet tanks (not the bowls), canned fruits and vegetables, and melting ice cubes from your refrigerator. Water heaters are another possible source.

- Try to avoid telephone use so that lines are open for emergency agencies.

- Whether you are at home or not at the time of the emergency, do not go outside if you suspect chemical, biological or radioactive contamination may be present. Wait for advice or possible evacuation orders from emergency personnel or from the Emergency Broadcast Network and be prepared to move immediately if advised to do so.

- If you are at home at the time of a chemical or radiation related emergency occurs and it is determined that outside contamination is a factor, immediately turn off air conditioning and close all doors and windows. Sealing windows and door jams with heavy duty duct tape is advised to help prevent contaminated particles from entering. Remain indoors until you have been otherwise advised by authorities or their order for evacuation is given.

- If a you are in a building where significant damage has occurred, immediately move to an area of safety and stay away from any fallen or broken electrical lines. If smoke is present, do not open any doors without ensuring that there is no fire on the other side. Check for this possibility by carefully feeling the door or the handle. If it is extremely hot, that's generally a good indication that it is unsafe to enter. Additionally, do not smoke or light matches or candles in the event a gas leak may be present.

- Regardless of your location, if you are witness to an emergency situation, immediately move to an area of safety and report the event to authorities as soon as you are able. If there are injured people and it is safe to do so, assist them to a safer area and administer first aid until emergency personnel arrive.

- All family members should be knowledgeable as to how and when utilities should be turned off in the event such action becomes necessary.

- Remember the First Aid motto: Check, Call, and Care. Check the scene for any possible safety concerns such as downed electrical lines and similar dangers. Check the victim (s) so that this information may be relayed to the emergency services dispatcher. Call 911 for emergency assistance as soon as you are able to do so, and then provide care to the victim(s) as you are able.

- Shock is a medical condition often seen in trauma victims. Symptoms include weakness (or feeling lightheaded) and confusion. If you encounter this, it is important to keep the victim warm and as comfortable as possible until help arrives.

- Always practice Universal or Standard Precautions for infection control. These require that you carefully wash your hands, including the use of a fingernail brush, after using the toilet, before and after handling food products, after public contact, or if any possible contamination is suspected. Additionally, handle any contaminated materials or clothing in a way that prevents the transfer of microorganisms. The use of disposable latex gloves is recommended for this purpose. Also, hold any contaminated material or clothing item away from your body and don't touch any other surfaces while transporting them. Clothing contaminated with blood or other body fluids, or with any suspected biological agents should be laundered using a bleach solution of one part bleach to 10 parts of water. Also, any surfaces contaminated with blood or other body fluids, as well as with any suspected biological agents, should be wiped with a bleach solution or other antibacterial agent. This should be allowed to remain on the area for at least 30 minutes before rinsing.

Based largely on experience with military personnel and their families abroad, experts report that Americans often tend to be very cautious immediately after an initial attack, but may then become lulled into a false sense of security if nothing further happens right away. Indeed, as we now know, it is during these seeming periods of inactivity that terrorists do their planning, surveillance and preparation. It's therefore prudent that we never let our guard down.

In discussing emergency preparedness, Rick Freed, former Community Fire Safety Education Officer for the Henderson, Nevada Fire Department, commented that "The hope, of course, is that you never have to use this information. But should an emergency ever arise, the goal of good preparedness planning and education is that you will be able to effectively respond to the crisis without even having to think about what you're doing. My hope is that you will become familiar enough with all this information that your 'auto-pilot' will kick in and you'll instinctively follow the necessary steps that will keep yourself and others alive."

If fully implemented, the information contained in this book will do much to keep Americans safe from the insidious threat of terrorism. It is based on expert advice and opinion, as well as on historical evidence. Most of us can avoid becoming a victim. The choice is ours.

KEEPING THE FAITH

"From Ground Zero I am having trouble seeing it, but I believe
that there is another light to follow ahead. It is a light for all nations,
and in this light there is no darkness at all. I am putting my feeble trust
in this light, day to day, sometimes hour to hour."

- The Rev. Joseph E. Griesedieck III
St. Thomas Church, Fifth Avenue, Manhattan

Following the September 11, 2001 attacks on America, fear and anger gripped its citizens and indeed those of all civilized countries. The attacks were vicious and were clearly an act of war. In the aftermath, a grieving nation struggled to come to terms with what happened.

In the midst of the tragedy, we saw great acts of heroism and bravery, and an inspiring sense of national unity and patriotism. The true meaning of the term "American Spirit" was demonstrated over and over again.

"I will never look at a firefighter the same way again", said Rev. Bill Hybels of Willow Creek Community Church in South Barrington, Illinois. "What is in someone, hundreds of them, to compel them to run into a burning building while everyone else is running out, just to save people they don't even know? Their bravery has become part of our collective national legacy. Their bravery dignifies us all."

Although a great many citizens had lost family, friends, and co-workers, they nonetheless hurriedly stepped in to help rescue workers with food, and clothing. Some held up large signs saying "Thank You" and other sincere statements of encouragement and praise. Across the country others rushed to donate their blood, their time, and their money to help victims of the attack.

Still, the effects of the shock were evident. People flocked to places of worship as never before, turning to religion to help them through this time of trial. In a brief 18 minutes, Americans had lost their sense of safety and security. The very symbols of American freedom and financial success had been desecrated and destroyed without warning. Moreover, more subtle attacks soon began appearing in the form of anthrax and other means. In private, many began wondering if they had the courage and the faith to sustain them through what lay ahead.

The Rev. Mary F. Harvey, of Grace United Church in St. Louis, in addressing this issue, expressed this thought following the attacks:" May we learn that courage is not the absence of fear, but the capacity to act in the presence of fear. Faith is not the absence of doubt, but the courage to believe in spite of doubt. Trust is not the absence of qualms, but the capacity to go forward in spite of misgivings."

"We admit that we thought we were brave. We thought we were strong, but we had not expected what has come upon us this week."

Following the attacks and subsequent events, the American Red Cross was flooded with calls and questions from people who were clearly despondent and afraid.

On their website (www.redcross.org), they explained that following such an ordeal it was not uncommon for people to exhibit the following:

- Sadness, including crying more easily or wanting to cry

- Anger

- Fear

- Grief

- Trouble falling asleep, staying asleep, or having nightmares

- Changes in appetite such as eating too much, or not being hungry

- Problems in school and having a hard time concentrating

- Feelings of being helpless

- Wanting to be alone more often than usual or not wanting to be alone at all

- Moodiness and irritability

The Red Cross assured people that these were all normal feelings which may come and go. They explained further that "If you have ever been involved in another type of disaster such as an earthquake, tornado, or flood, you may find yourself remembering that disaster and feeling the same emotions you felt then."

Suggestions such as "talking it out" with a trusted person or relative, spending time with family, and doing something that could help others such as taking a First Aid or CPR class were recommended. They also urged asking for help if you feel you need it.

The Red Cross suggested that you "remind yourself of other times when you were afraid. Remember that you were able to deal with that fear and that it doesn't last forever."

Pastor Hilda G. Pecoraro, of the Green Valley Presbyterian Church in Henderson, Nevada encouraged her congregation to remember that "We believe that life overcomes death, that love is stronger than hatred, that light dispels darkness, and that hope conquers despair."

A recent Gallup Poll indicated that for 27% of those questioned, the terrorist attacks and resulting fear of the unknown had triggered them to make lifestyle changes. If anything, times of uncertainty or crisis provide each of us the opportunity for personal and spiritual growth. More importantly, perhaps, they help us to redefine those things in our lives which are truly the most valuable. Family, friends, the little rituals, and sometimes even the mundane activities of daily life take on new meaning.

In their USA WEEKEND article, "Souls of Steel", Cokie and Steven V. Roberts provided an interesting analogy. "Think of how steel is made," they said. "Like steel, our spirit is stronger than iron because the steelmaking process adds alloys to the basic element found in nature, and then tempers them under fire to create a new, harder substance. In the process of making the American spirit, alloys of virtue and memory, heroism and hardship, are continually added to the raw materials of America's past and fused in the forge of history."

Holocaust survivors and former prisoners of war have often described how, in their darkest hours, just thinking about their homes and their families, their country, and sometimes the very concept of freedom itself often kept them from losing their sanity and gave them the will to keep living.

One man recalled that during his childhood his father would often take him for evening walks around the neighborhood. It was their special time together, away from his older brothers and sisters. Years later, as a prisoner of war, the vivid memory of the sights and enticing aromas wafting from the homes and kitchens of the ethnically diverse area sustained him through his time of crisis. And, he emphasized, the love of his family kept him strong.

Another man recalled how the determination to somehow rescue his young wife from the separate concentration camp where she was being held became the driving force that helped him endure considerable pain, depravation, and hardship. Years later, as the two sat together in the small apartment of the assisted living facility where they lived, his wife recalled how each night after she prayed, she closed her eyes tight and tried to send him "mental messages" of love. "When the war broke out and all this happened," she said, "we never lost our faith in God. We never did."

Deep religious faith and strong convictions have carried many through times of war and crisis. In fact, a story exists about the commanding officer of a World War I army battalion who insisted that his men memorize the 91st Psalm. In spite of incredible

odds and often harrowing experiences, everyone of his men survived the war.

In moving from fear to faith, we need to keep in mind that we Americans have

always shown a great resiliency. From our forefathers who built this country to those

succeeding generations who battled long and hard to keep us free, we have survived

wars and multiple hardships to build a great country that is still the envy of all other

nations.

America is now facing a tremendous challenge of her strength, her courage, and

her resolve. As this generation is learning, the freedom that we have so often taken

for granted brings with it a great price and that price is personal and collective

responsibility. At the same time, it's important to keep things in perspective. Douglas

S. Derrer, in his book We Are All The Target, pointed out that more Americans are

killed annually in traffic accidents and homicides than by terrorists. And, as U.S.

Attorney General John Ashcroft emphasized, we need to place our focus on general

preparedness as opposed to paralysis.

"Freedom and fear are at war," President Bush said in addressing the nation.

"The advance of human freedom, the great achievement of our time and the great

hope of every time, now depends on us."

Throughout history, war and violence have plagued mankind. In spite of our

seeming social progress and technological advances, these things continue today. Yet in looking back through history, what has often separated victory from defeat, has been the unity, the resolute action, and the strength and courage of a nation's people. That was clearly demonstrated during the American Revolutionary War, and again with the French and British during World War II. Certainly there are other well-documented instances, as we know. The difference today is that terrorism is so new to Americans. It's very nature brings with it a great sense of dread and uncertainty. It is nonetheless something with which we are having to deal.

During World War I and World War II, strong leadership and resolute action by the United States and the allied nations were responsible in large part for the victories that took place and the freedoms that we continue to enjoy. But private citizens also played a major role, as well. We saw examples of this in the various underground and resistance movements during those periods, as well as in other not so well-known endeavors. These individuals exhibited great patriotism, bravery and perseverance. The recent attacks on this country were a clarion bell and now, it appears, America's citizens are being called upon to do the same.

Jon Meacham, in Time magazine's commemorative Fall 2001 issue, reported on a White House Christmas eve celebration that took place in 1941. America had been at war for a mere three weeks following the Japanese attack on Pearl Harbor. Joining President Franklin Roosevelt in the lighting of the Christmas tree on the South Lawn was his friend Winston Churchill. On that night, Meacham stated, Churchill made the following remark: "Let the children have their night of fun and laughter. Let the gifts

of Father Christmas delight their play. Let us grown-ups share to the full in their

unstinted pleasures before we turn again to the stern task and formidable years that lie

before us, resolved that, by our sacrifice and daring, these same children will not be

robbed of their inheritance or denied the right to live in a free and decent world."